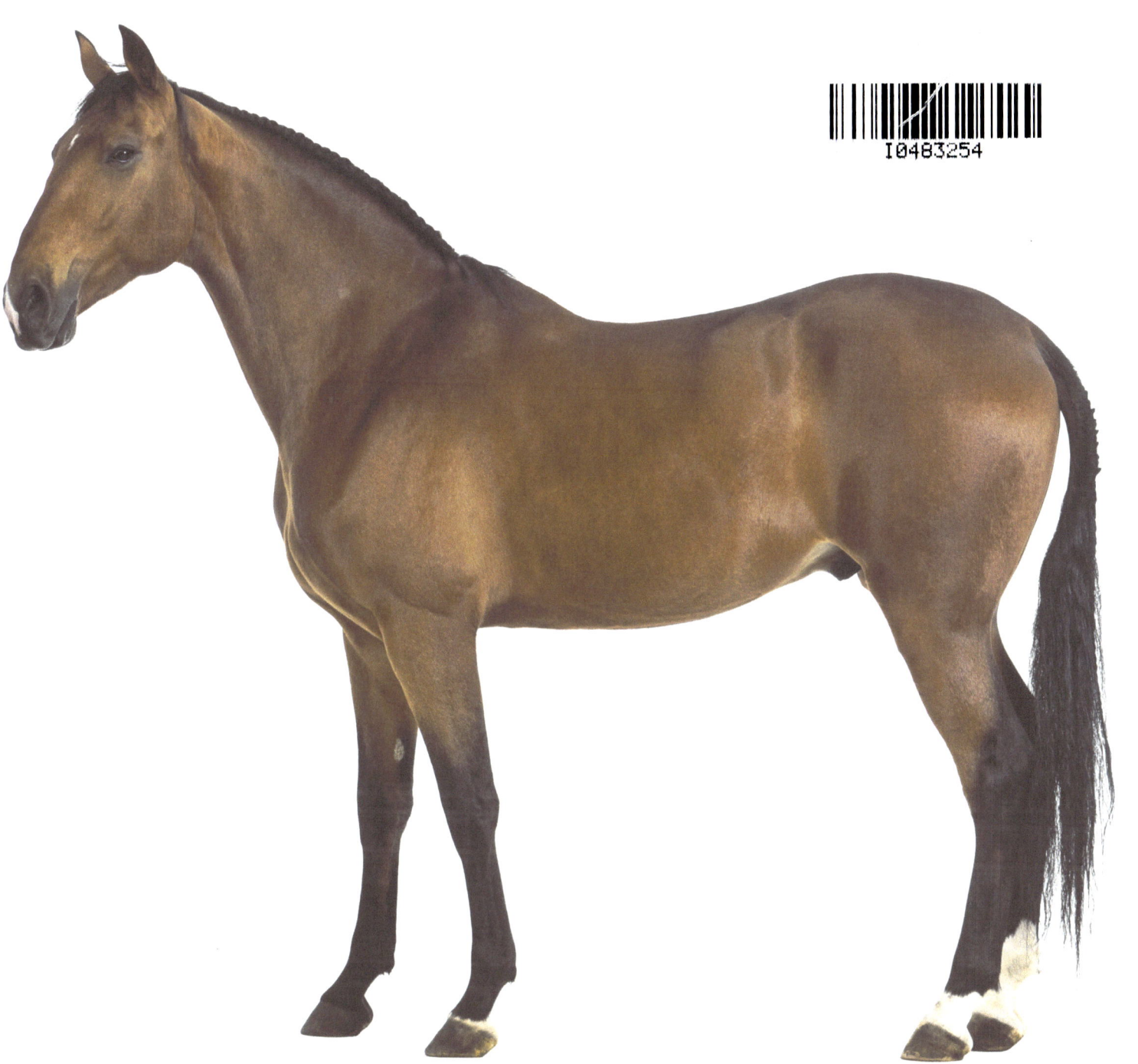

BAY ANDALUSIAN GELDING

*Isolated*

# HORSE

*Images for Artist's Reference & Inspiration*

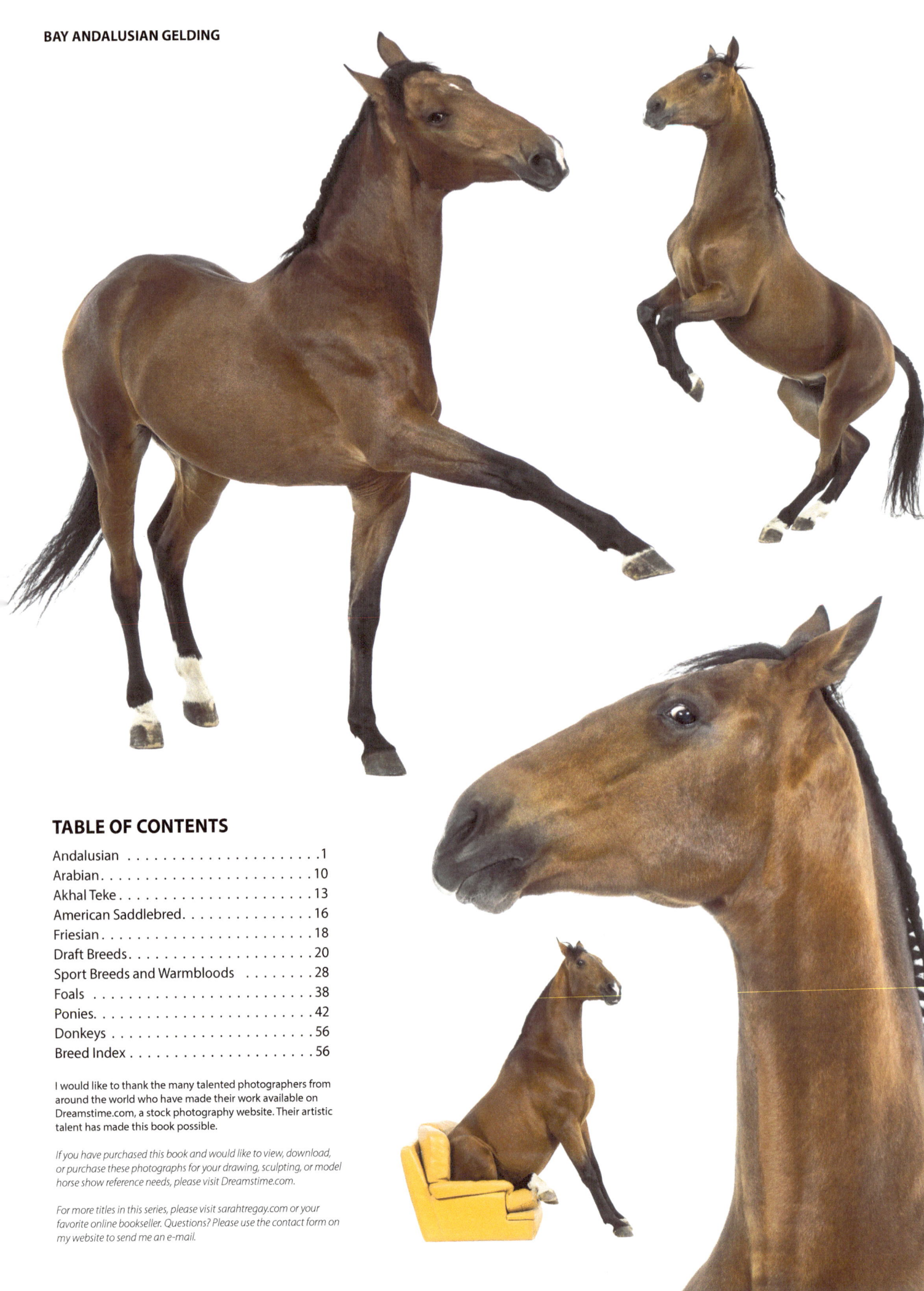

**BAY ANDALUSIAN GELDING**

## TABLE OF CONTENTS

I would like to thank the many talented photographers from around the world who have made their work available on Dreamstime.com, a stock photography website. Their artistic talent has made this book possible.

*If you have purchased this book and would like to view, download, or purchase these photographs for your drawing, sculpting, or model horse show reference needs, please visit Dreamstime.com.*

*For more titles in this series, please visit sarahtregay.com or your favorite online bookseller. Questions? Please use the contact form on my website to send me an e-mail.*

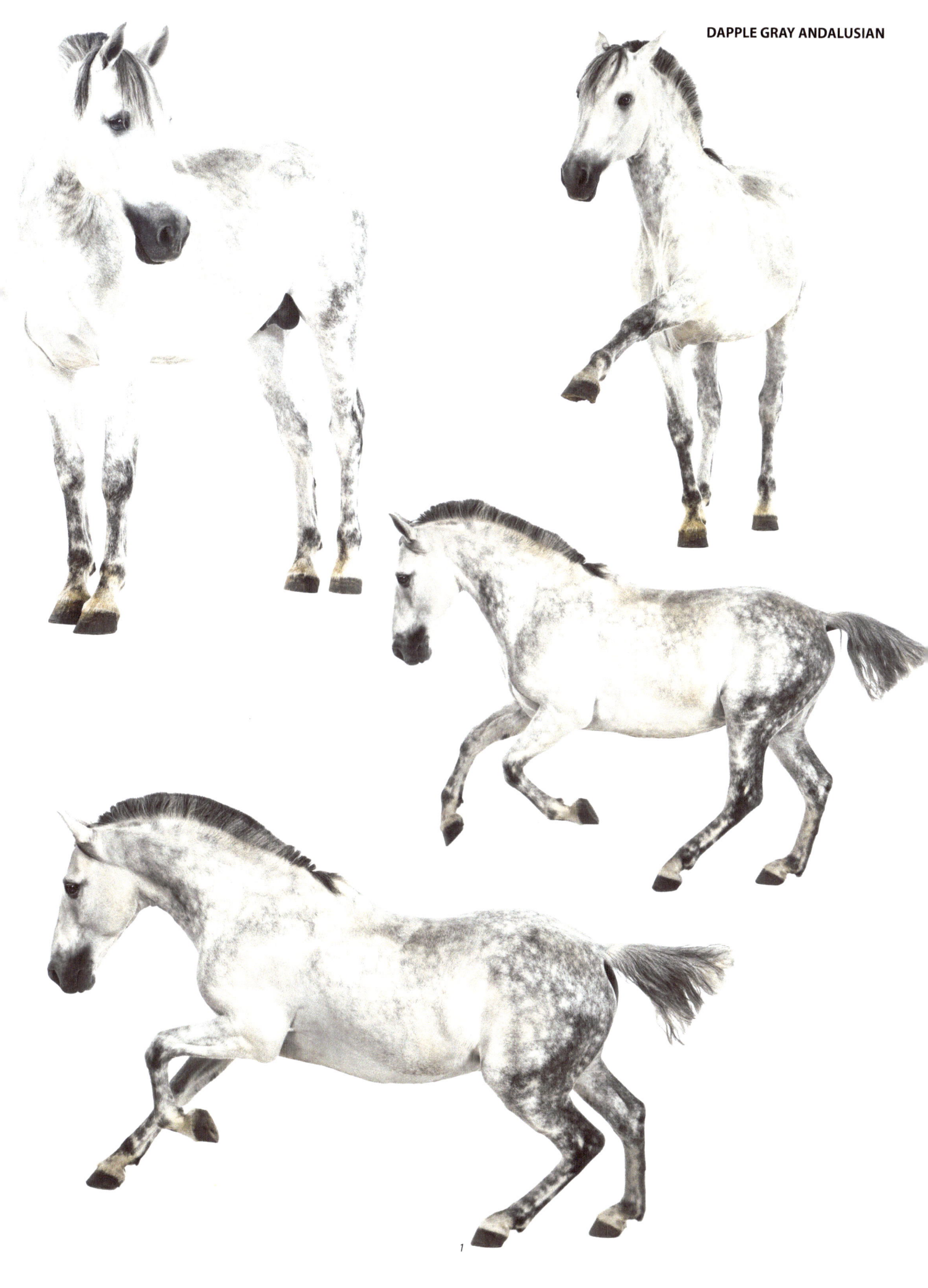

**DAPPLE GRAY ANDALUSIAN**

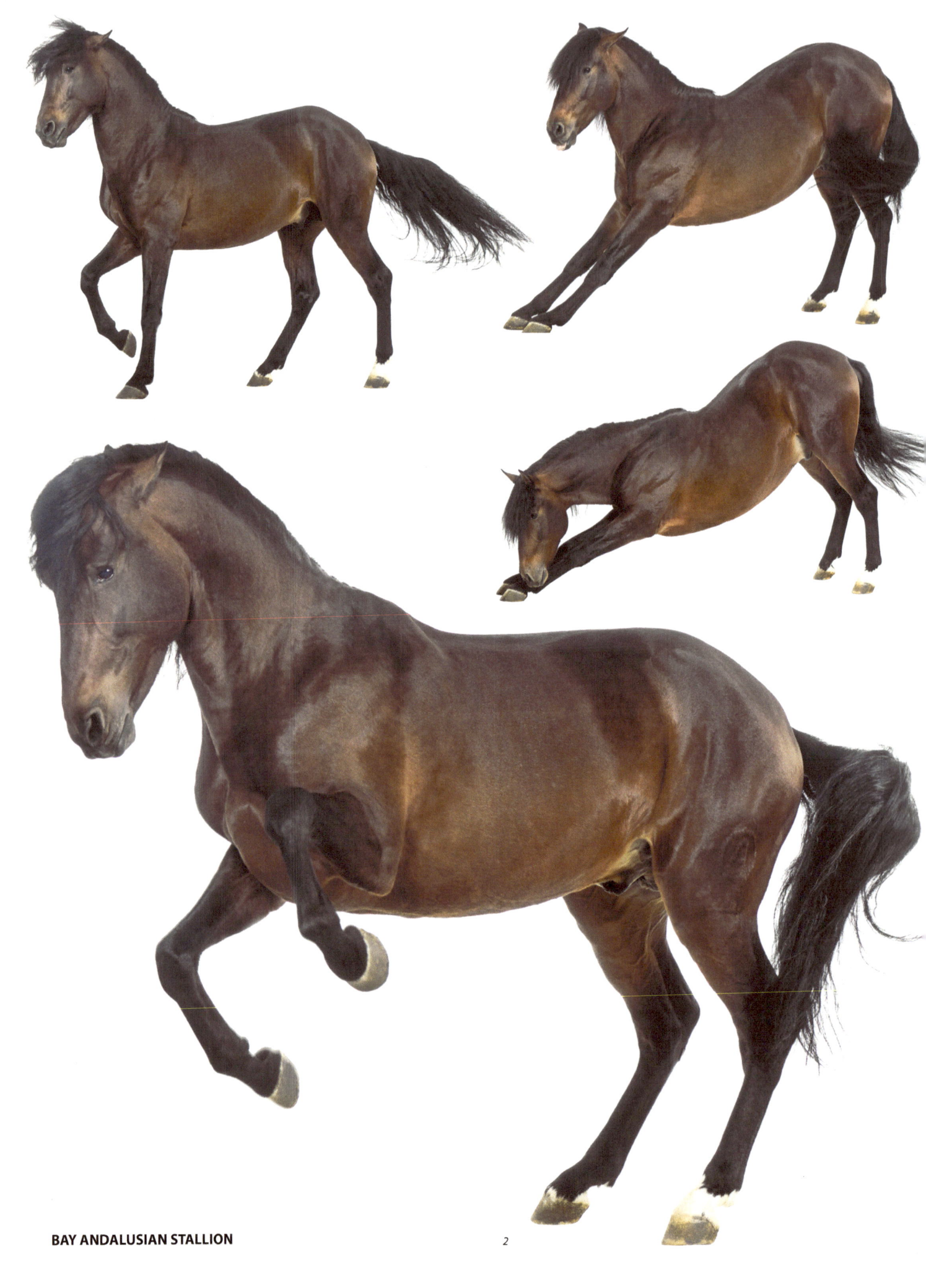

**BAY ANDALUSIAN STALLION**

2

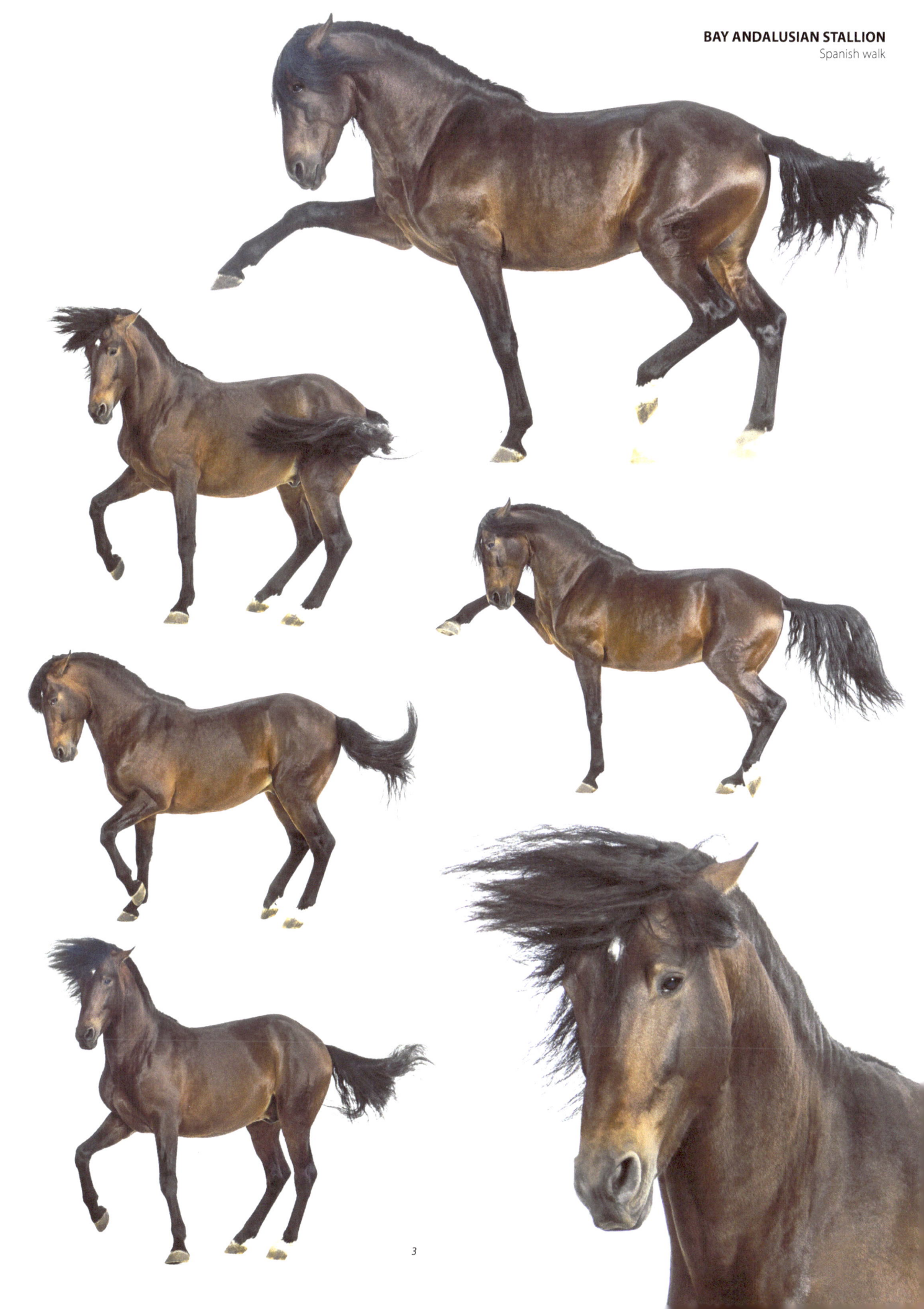

3

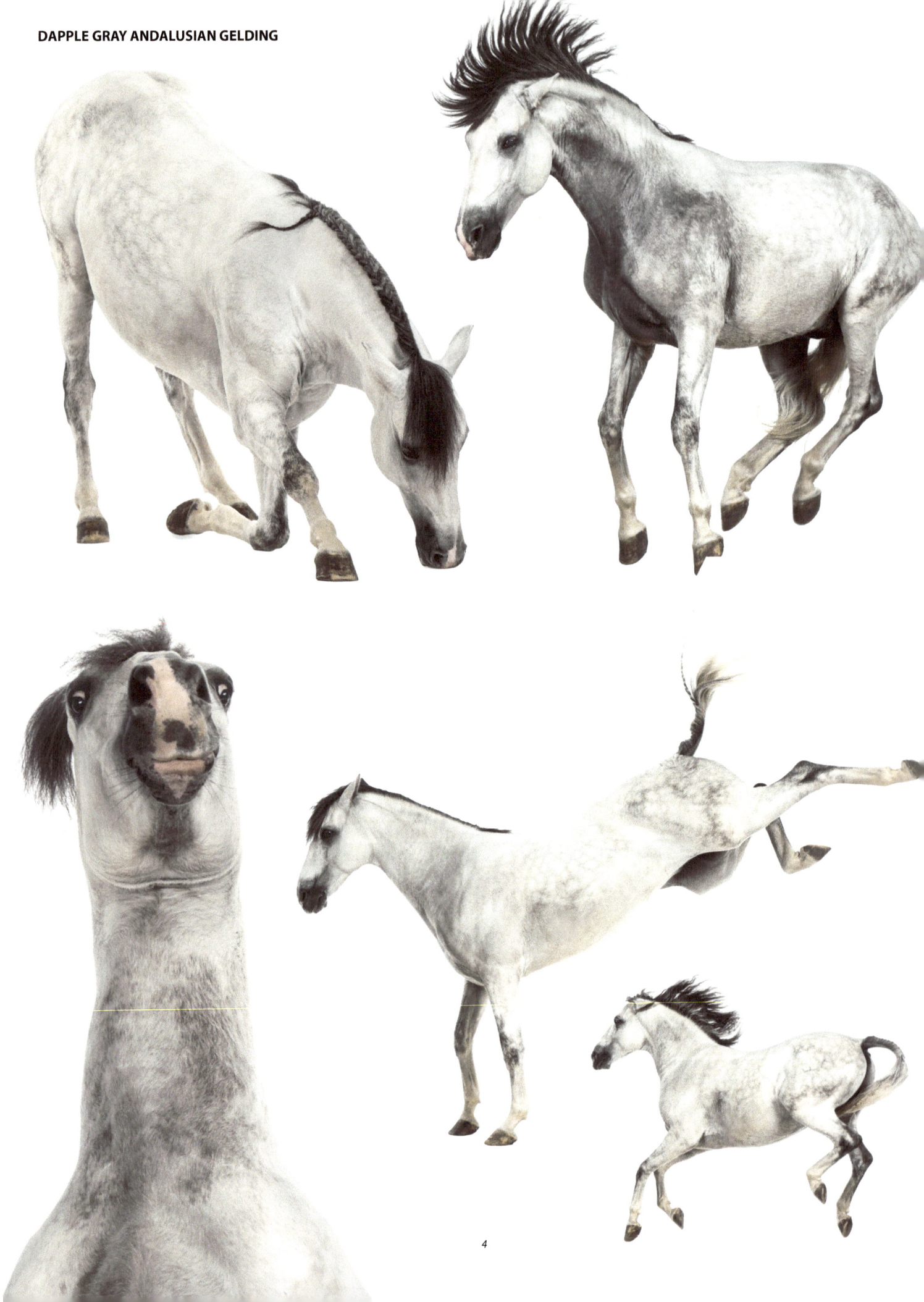

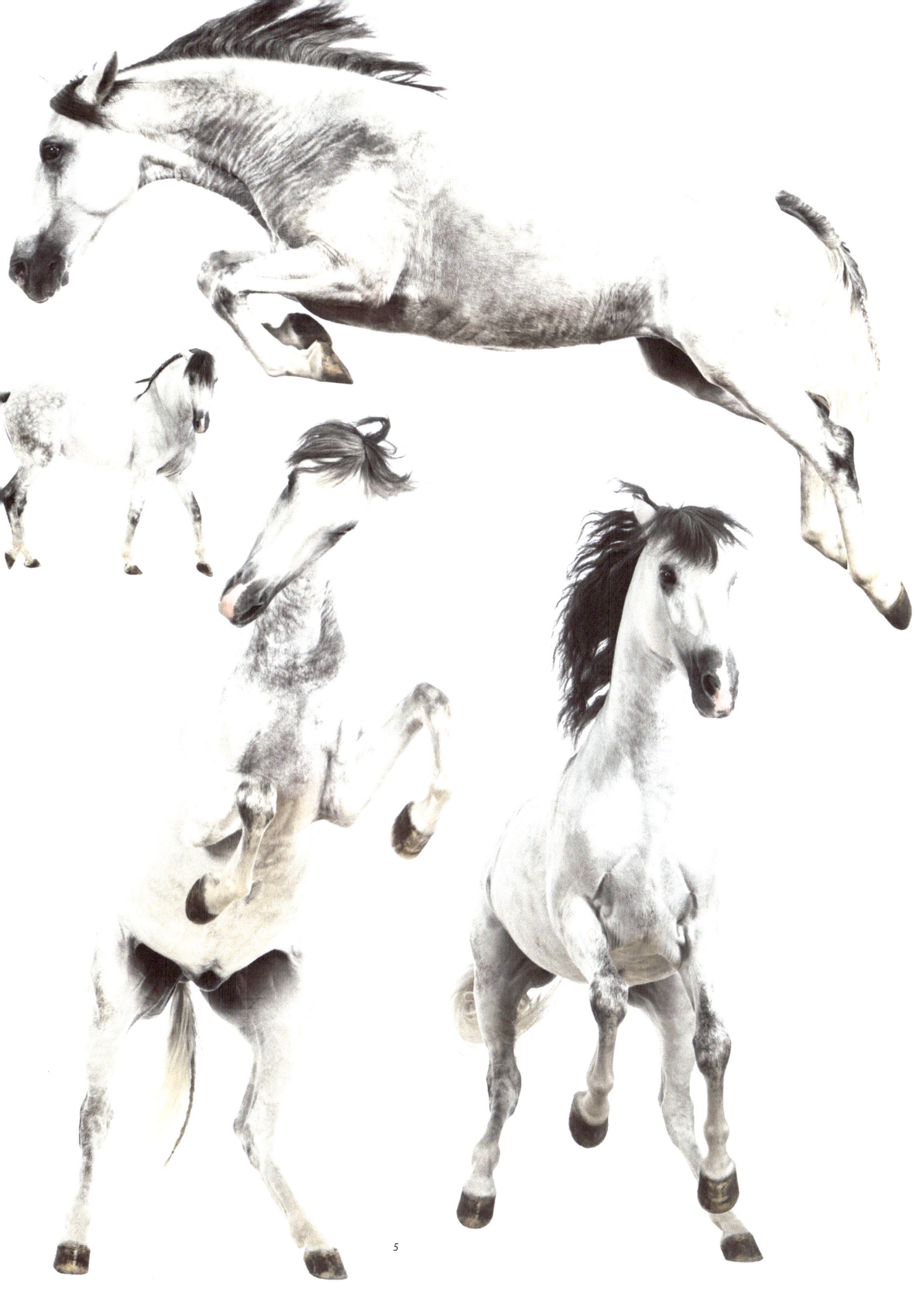

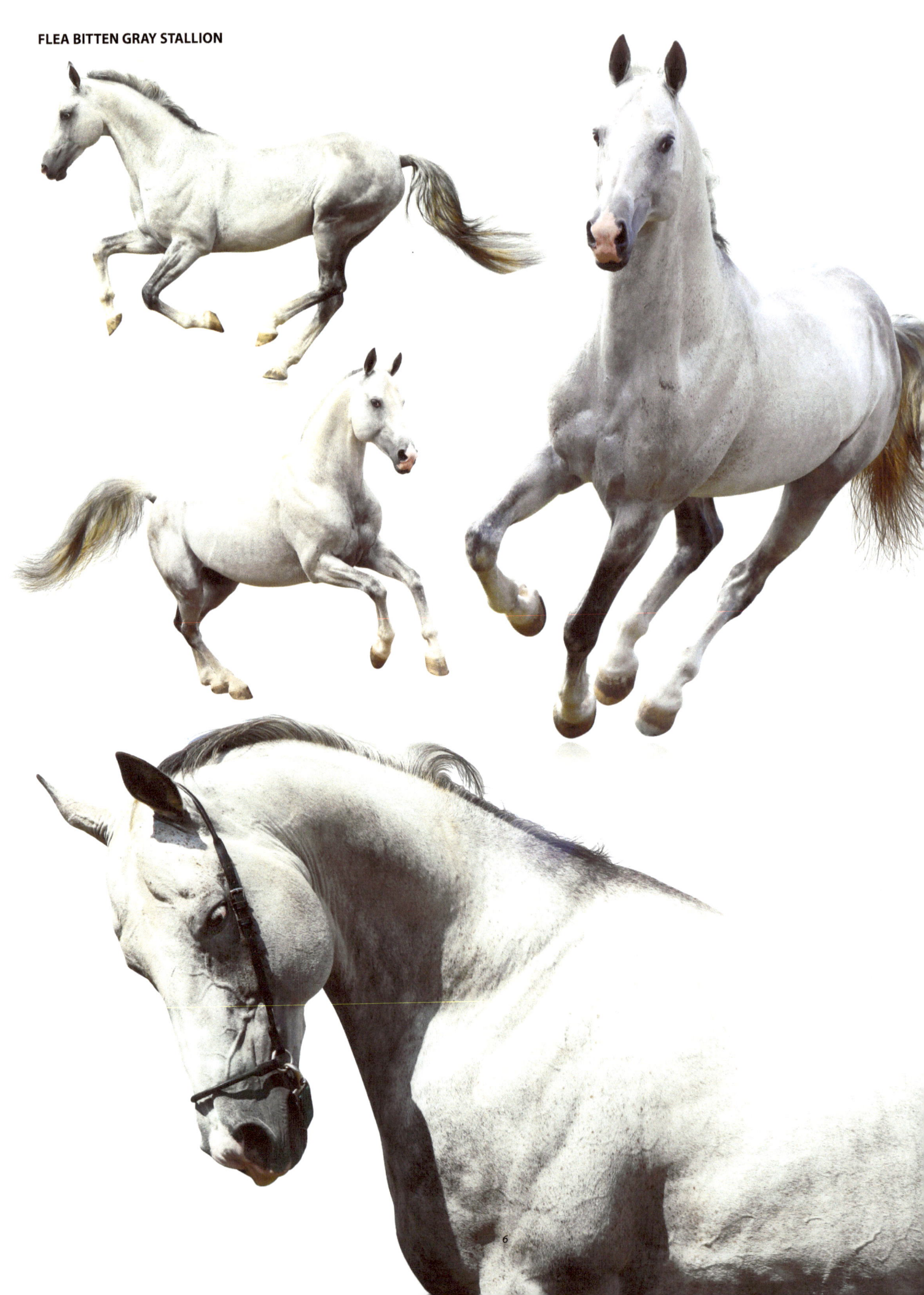

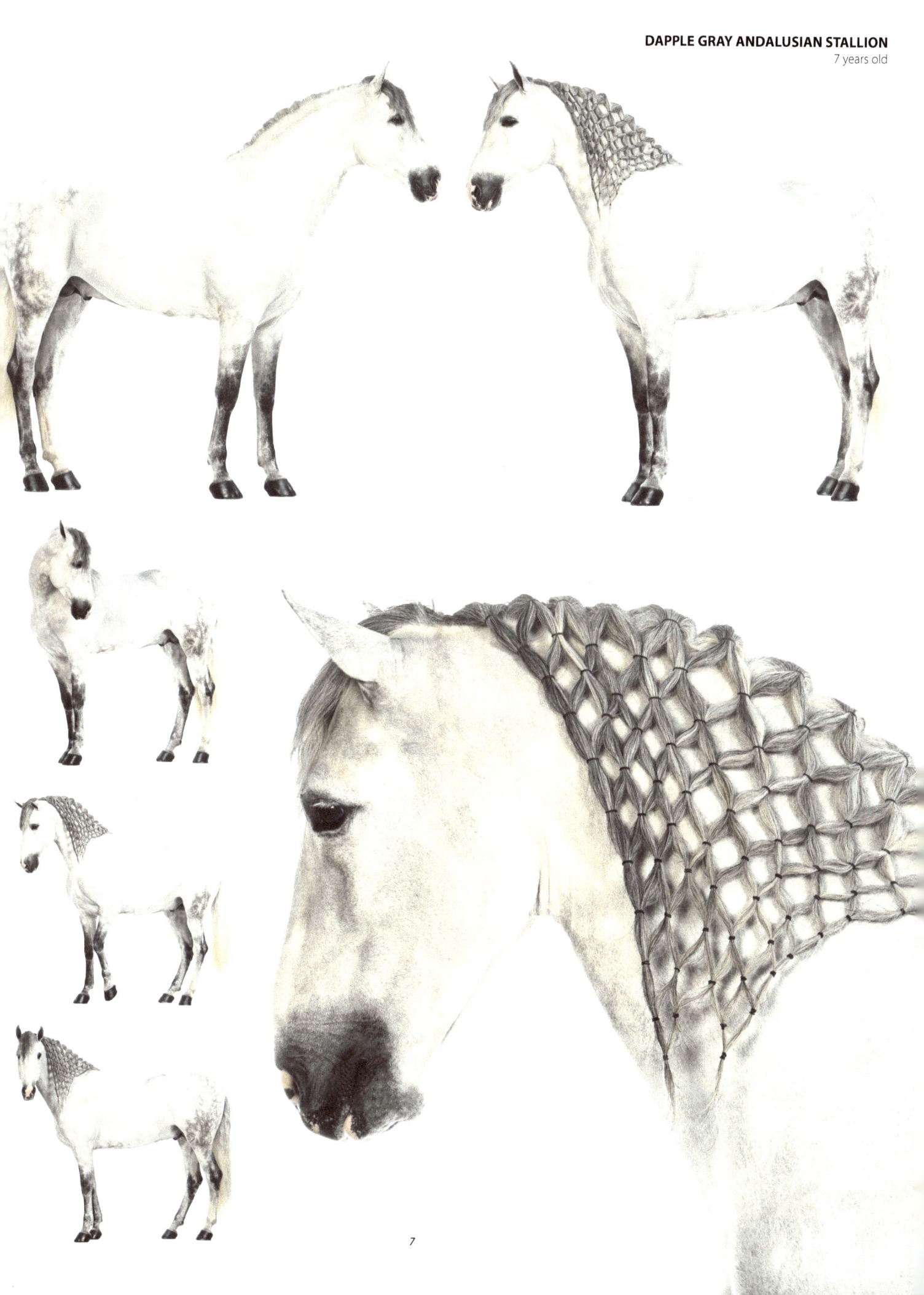

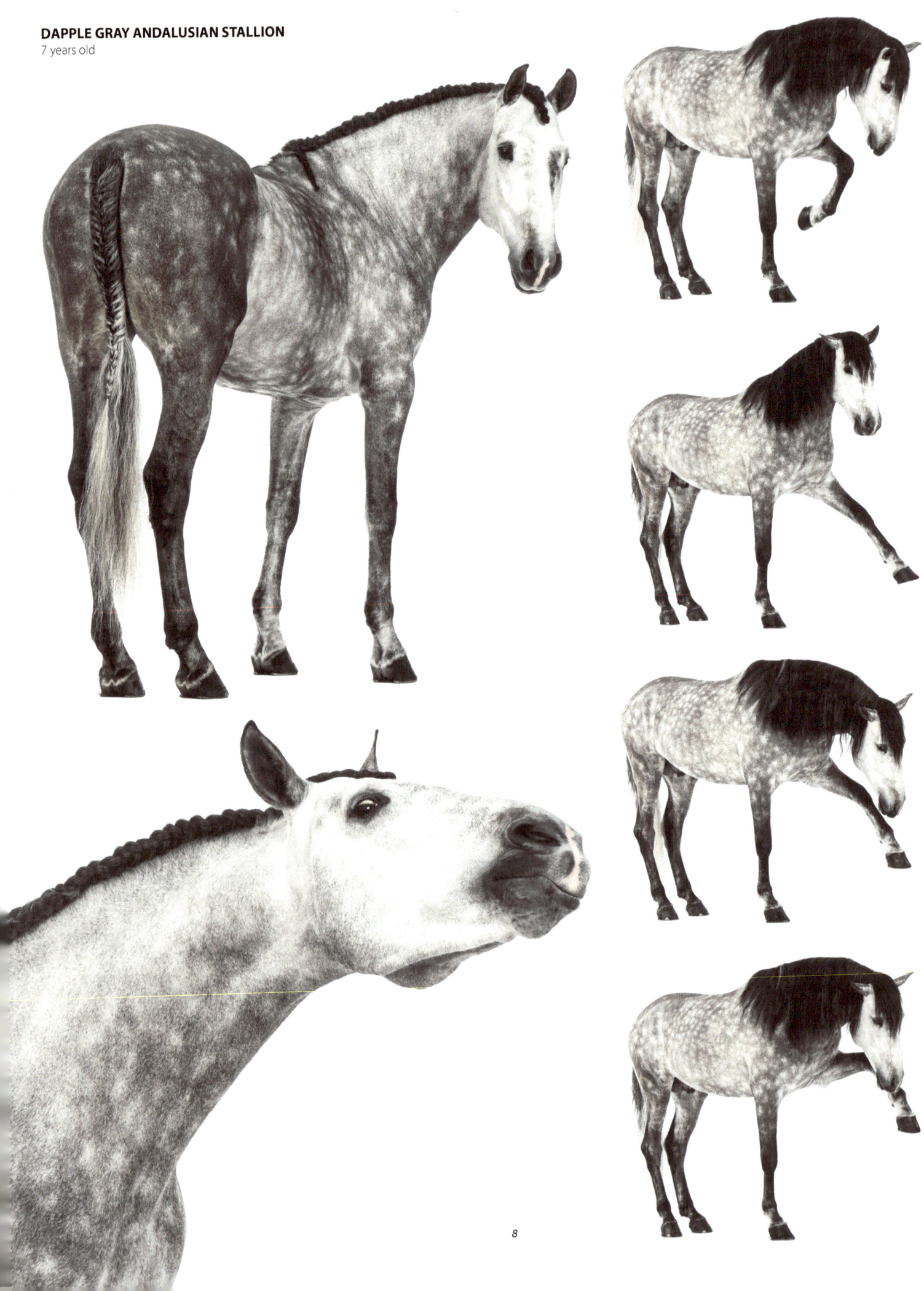

8

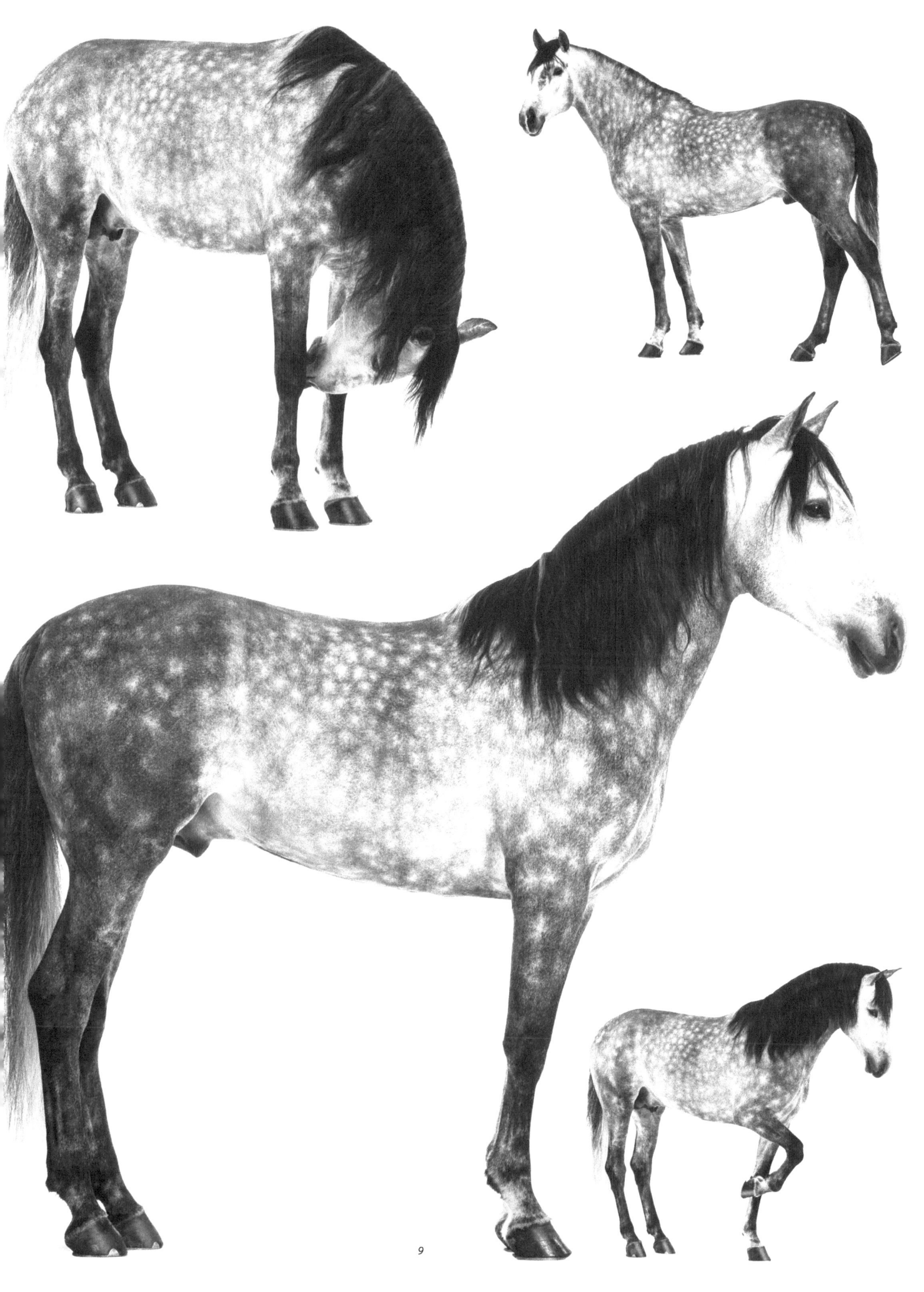

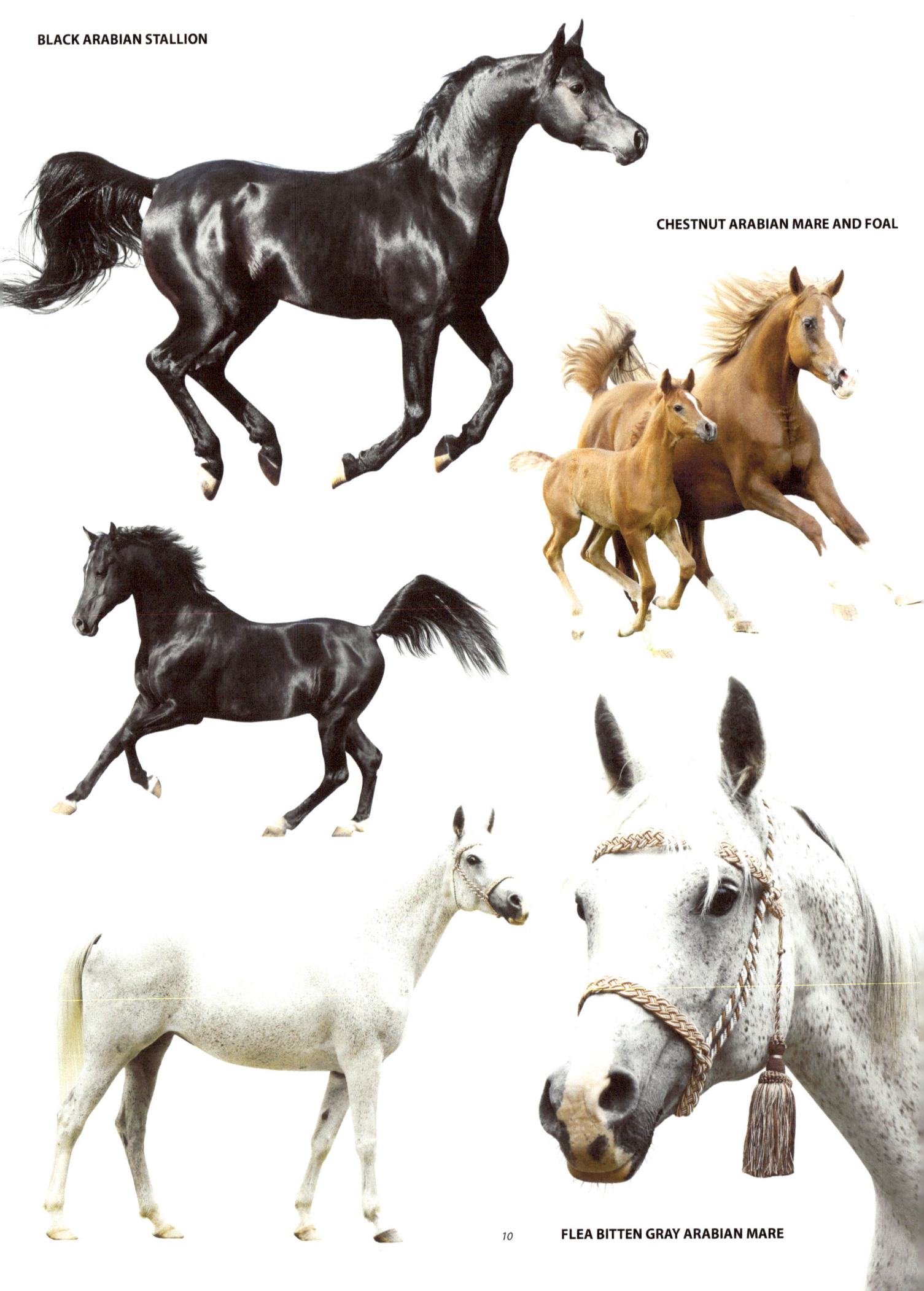

BLACK ARABIAN STALLION

CHESTNUT ARABIAN MARE AND FOAL

FLEA BITTEN GRAY ARABIAN MARE

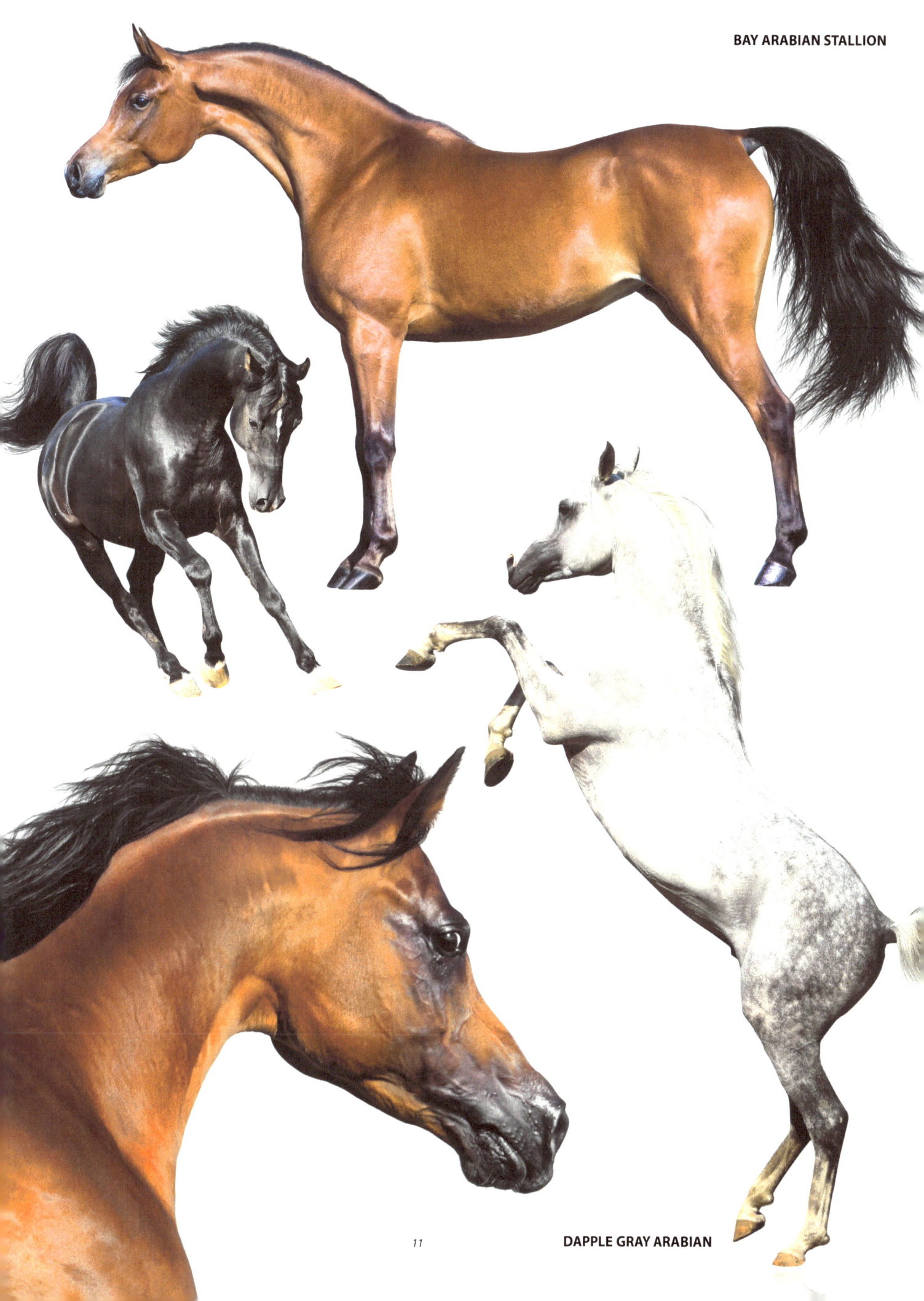

DAPPLE GRAY ARABIAN

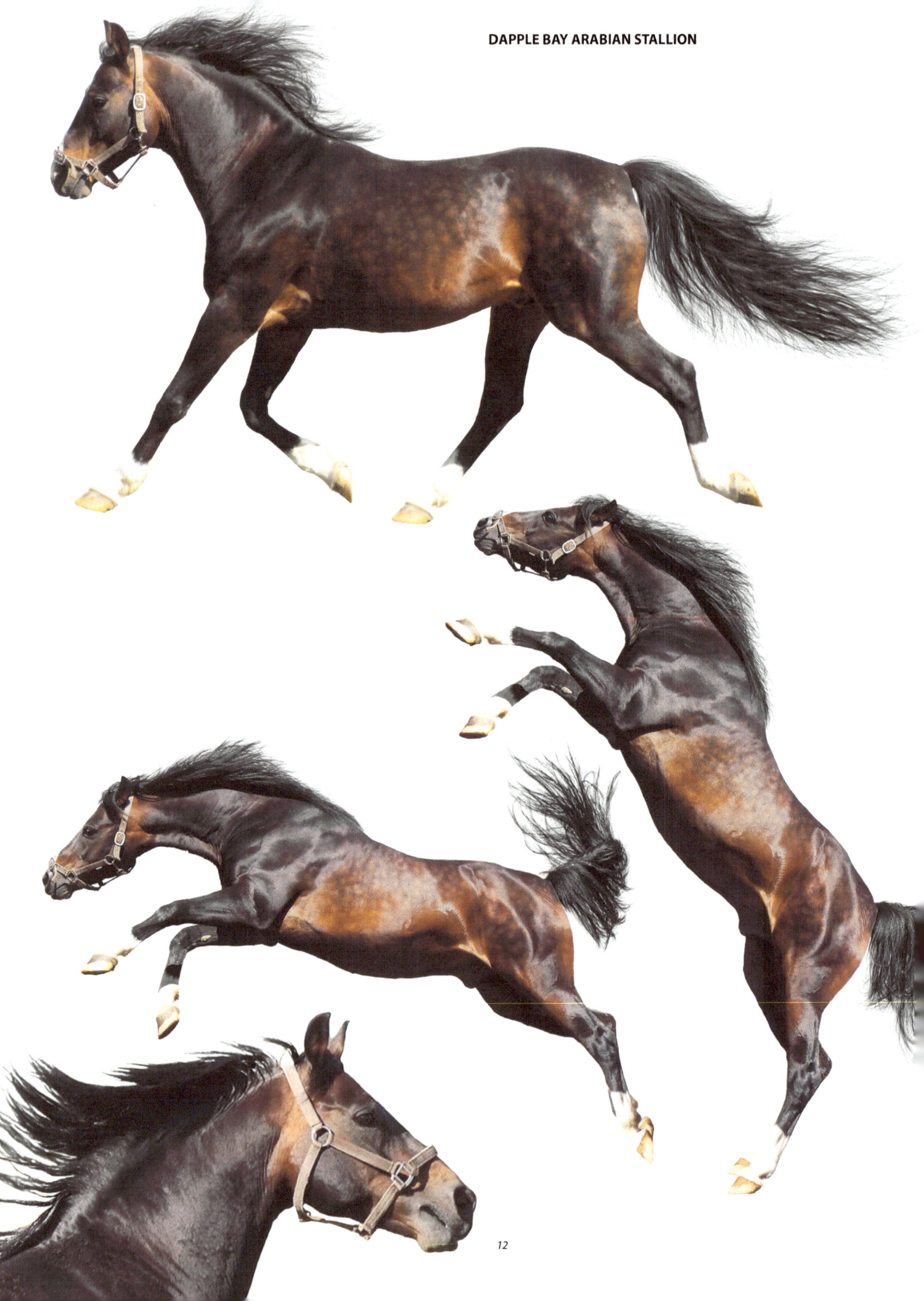

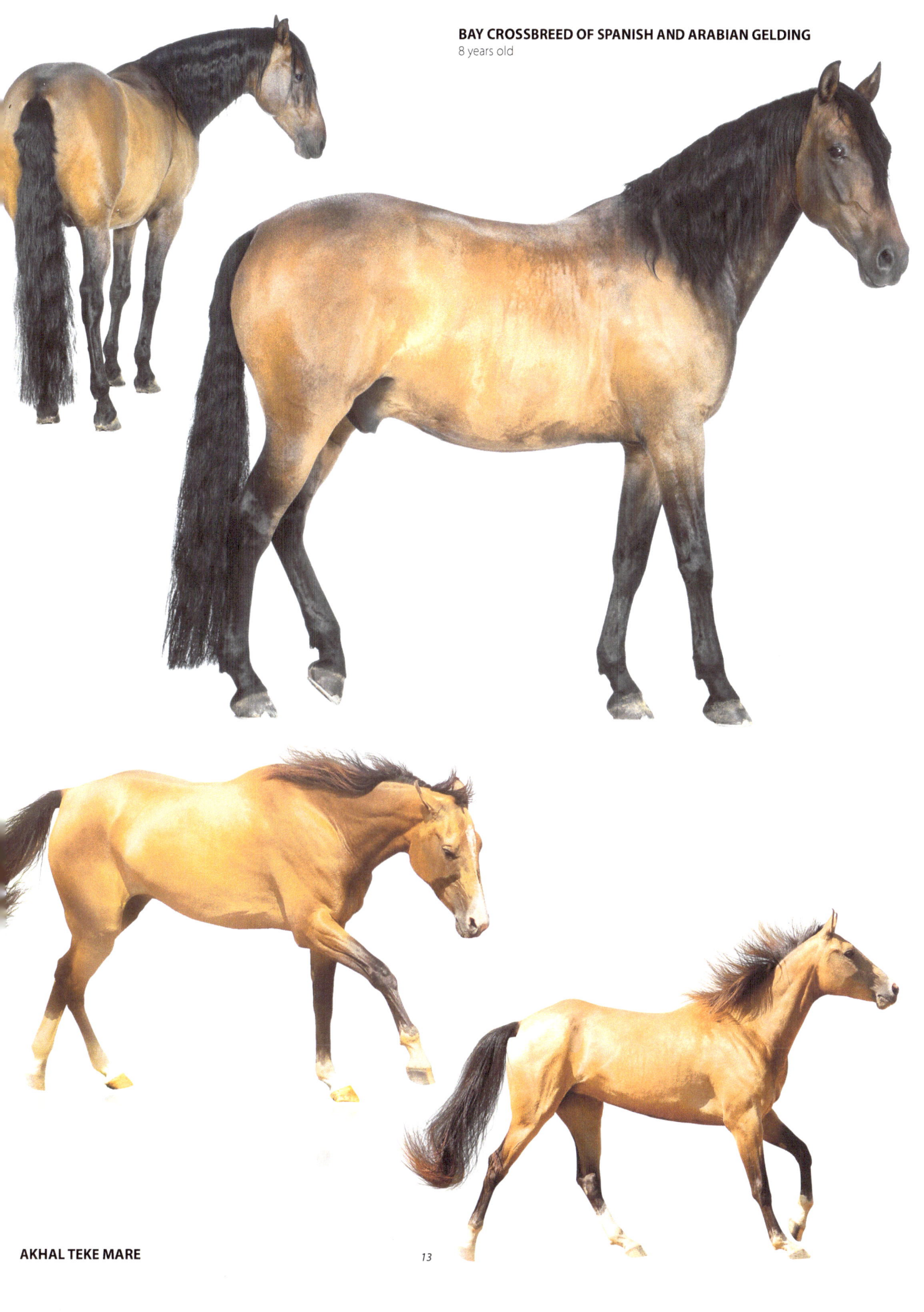

**BAY CROSSBREED OF SPANISH AND ARABIAN GELDING**
8 years old

**AKHAL TEKE MARE**

13

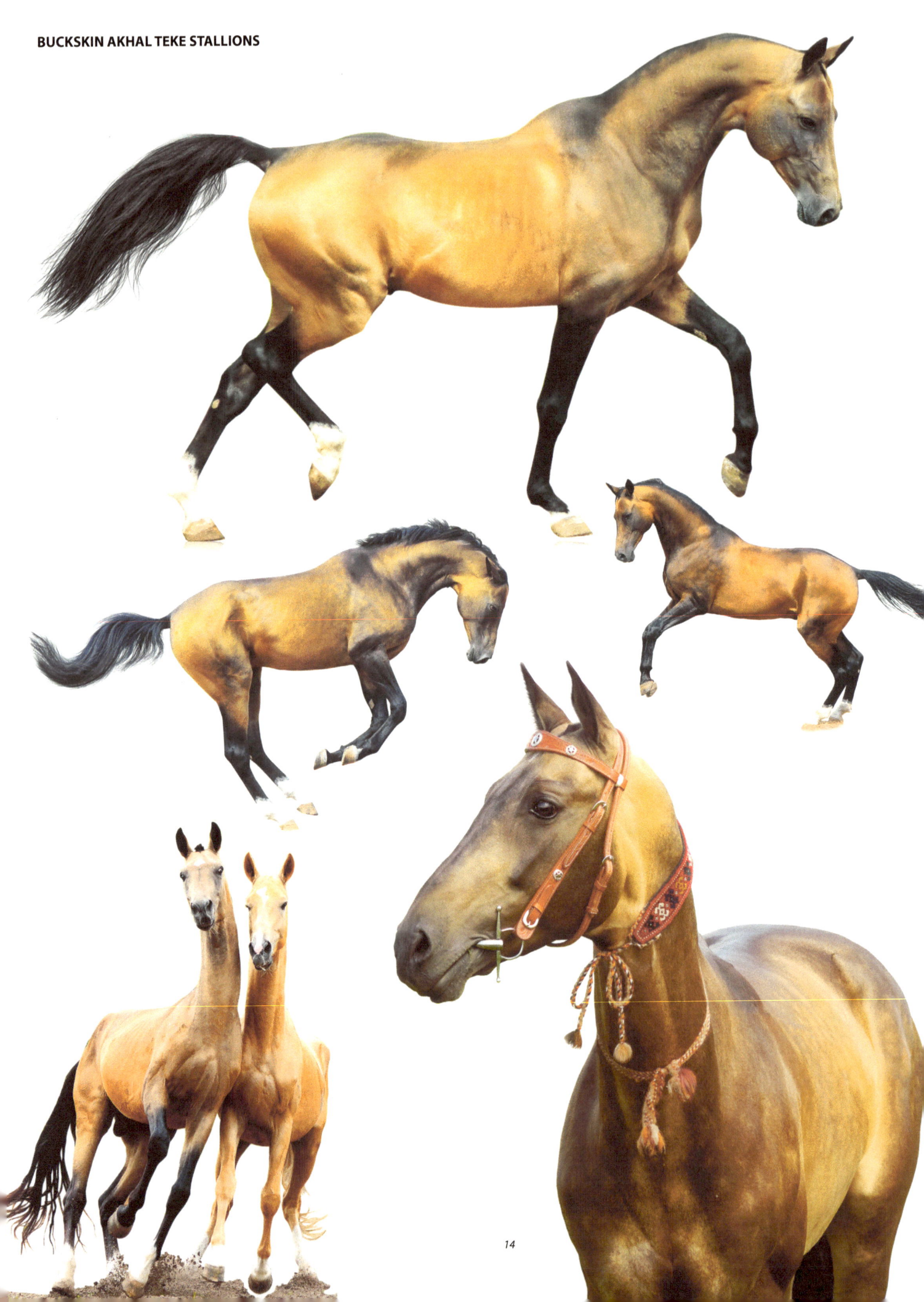

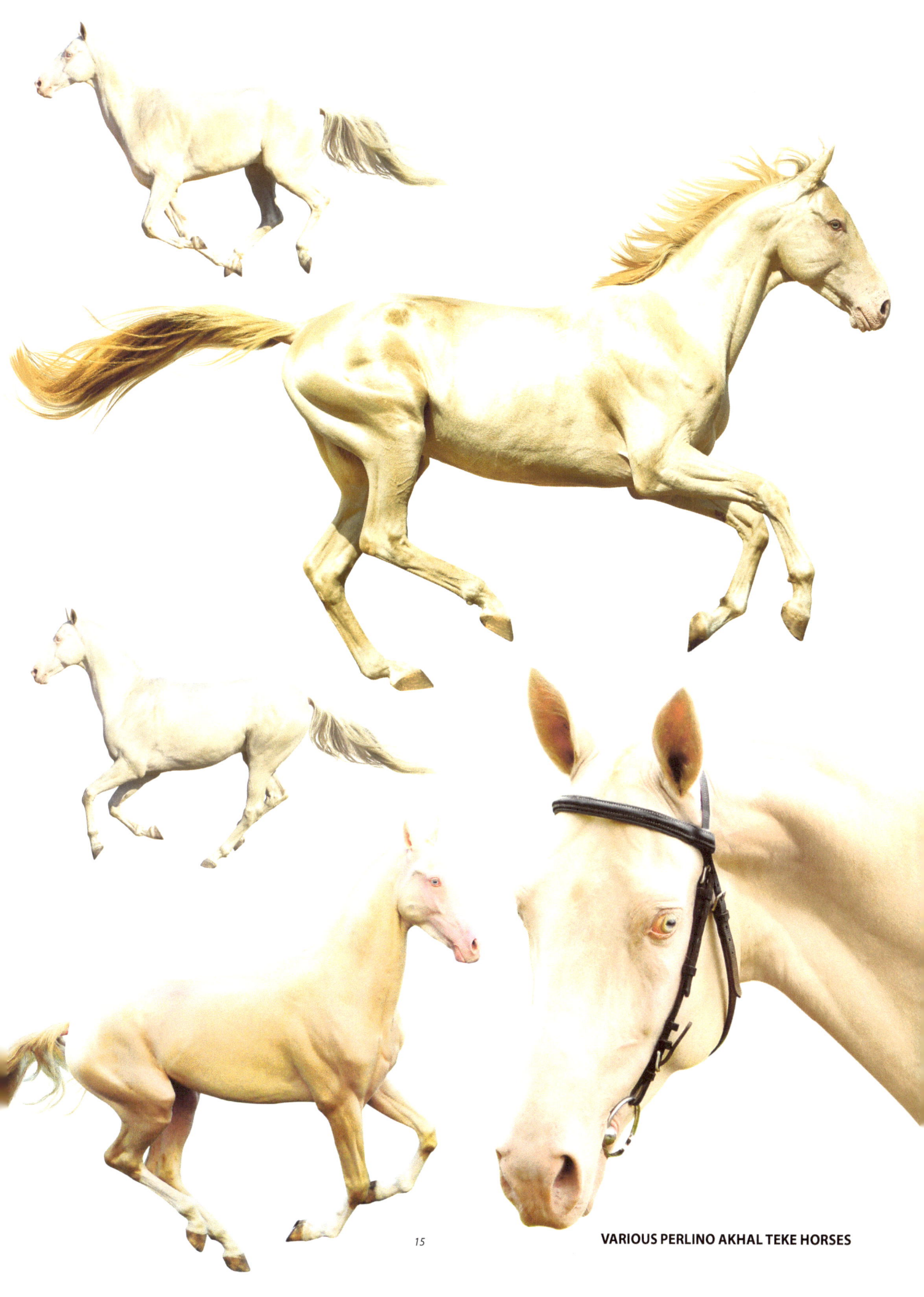

**VARIOUS PERLINO AKHAL TEKE HORSES**

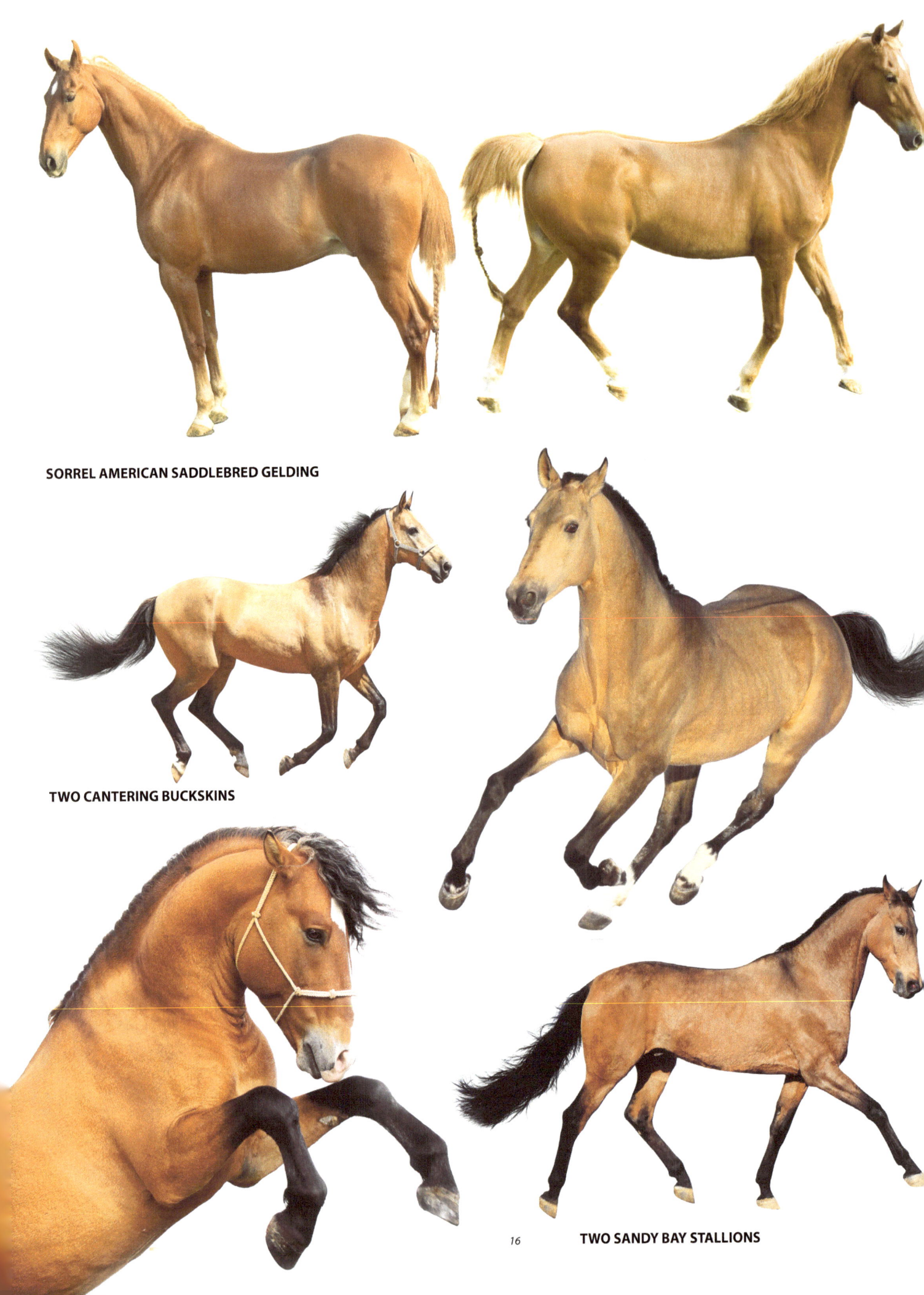

SORREL AMERICAN SADDLEBRED GELDING

TWO CANTERING BUCKSKINS

TWO SANDY BAY STALLIONS

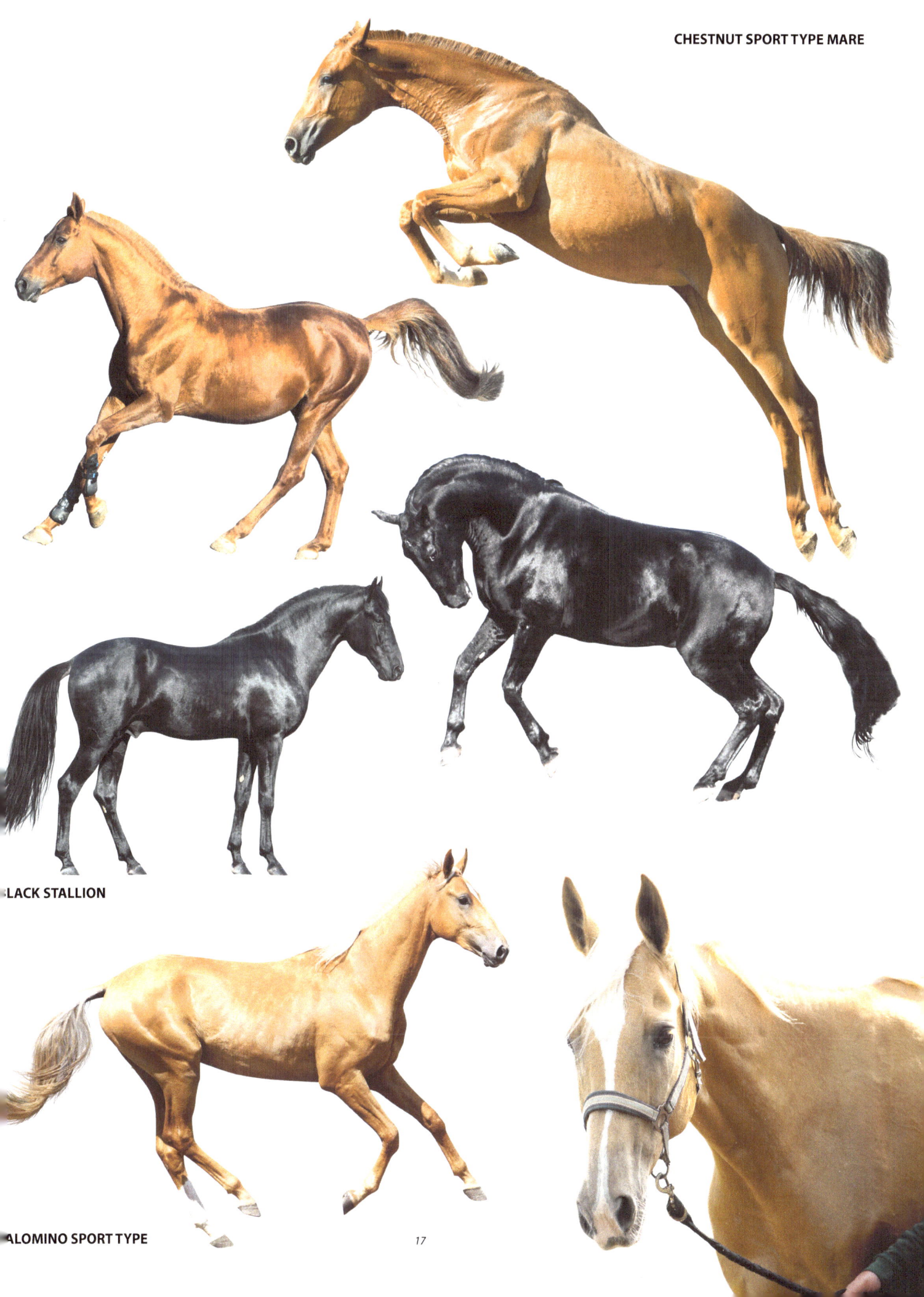

CHESTNUT SPORT TYPE MARE

LACK STALLION

ALOMINO SPORT TYPE

17

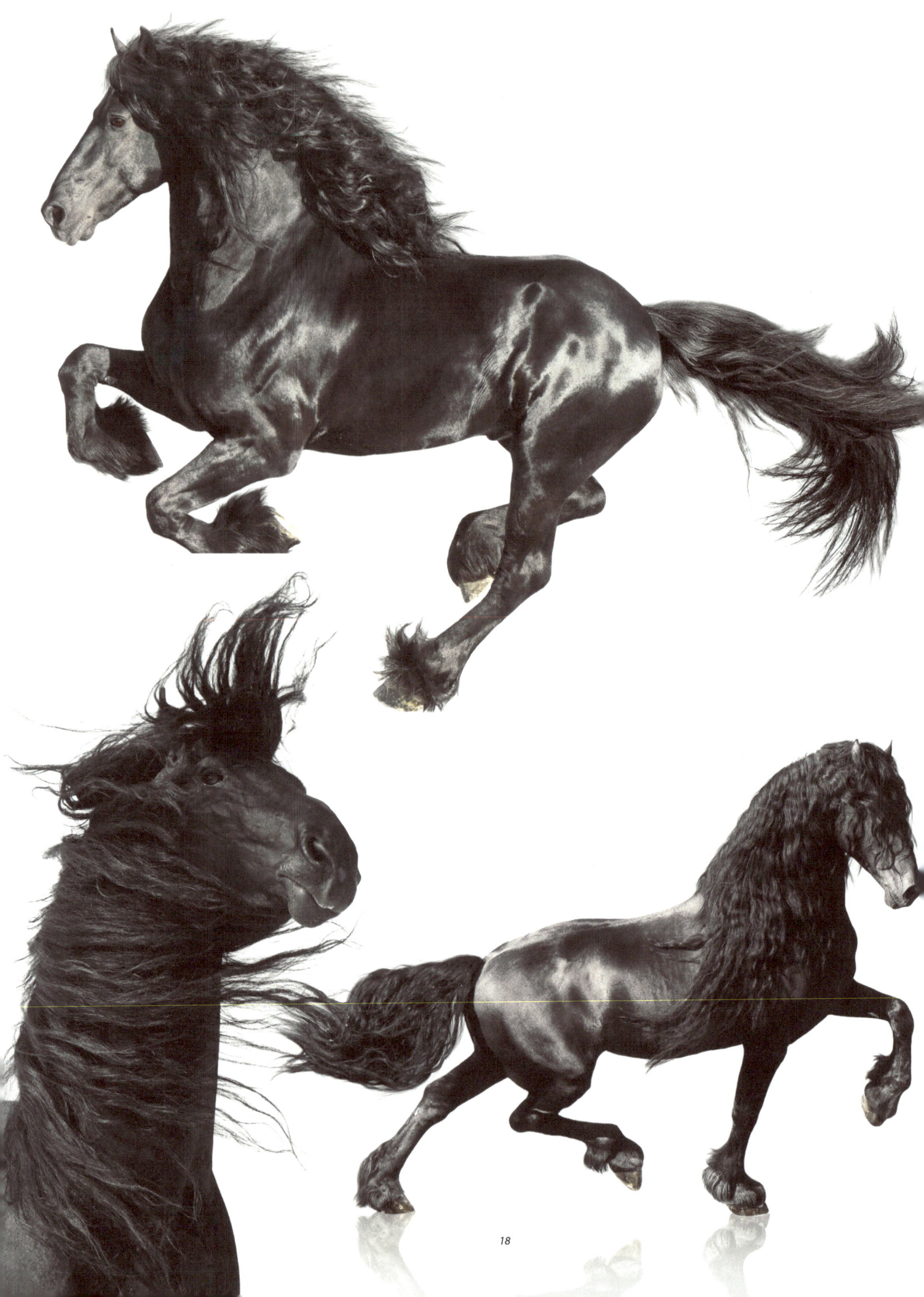

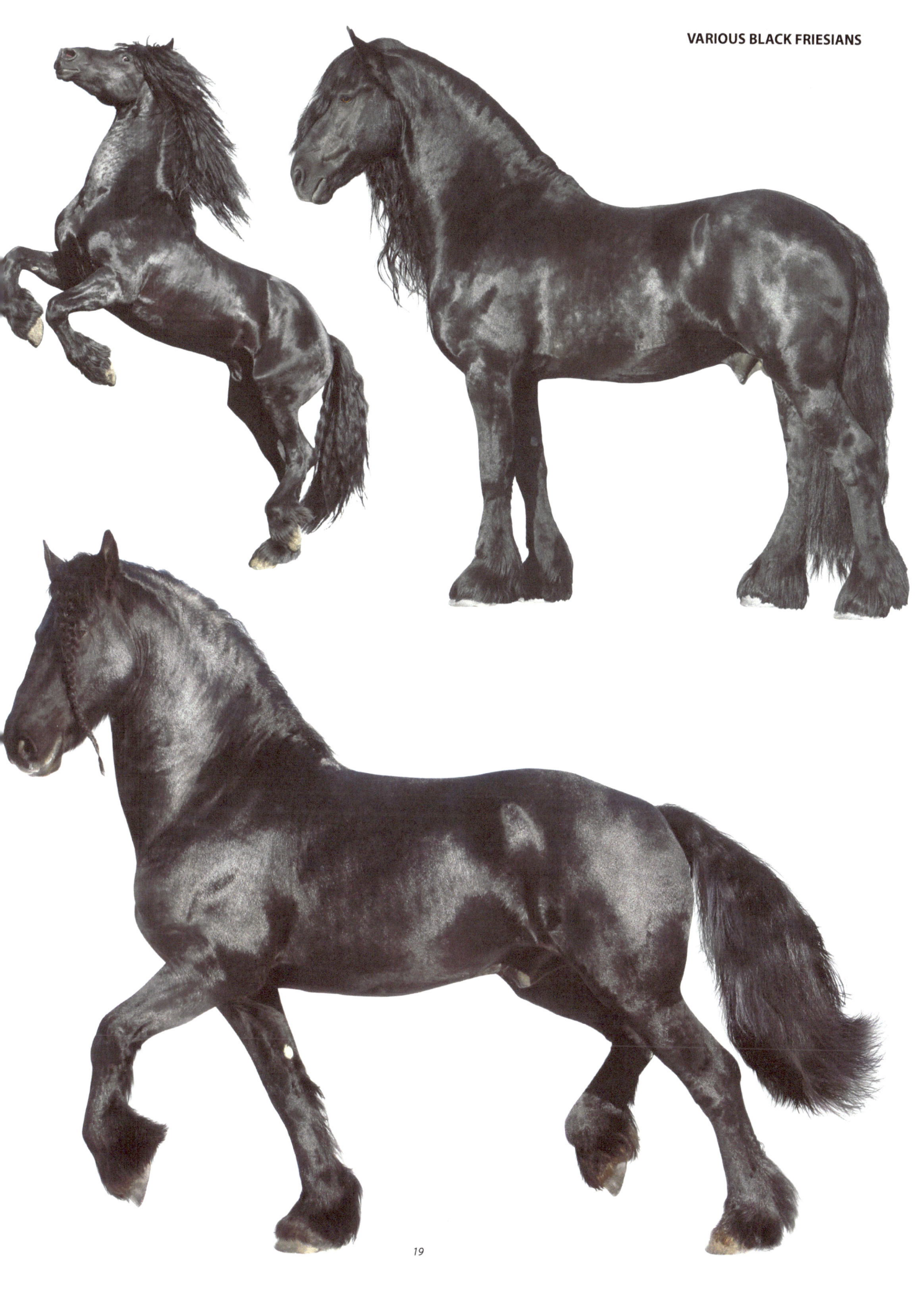

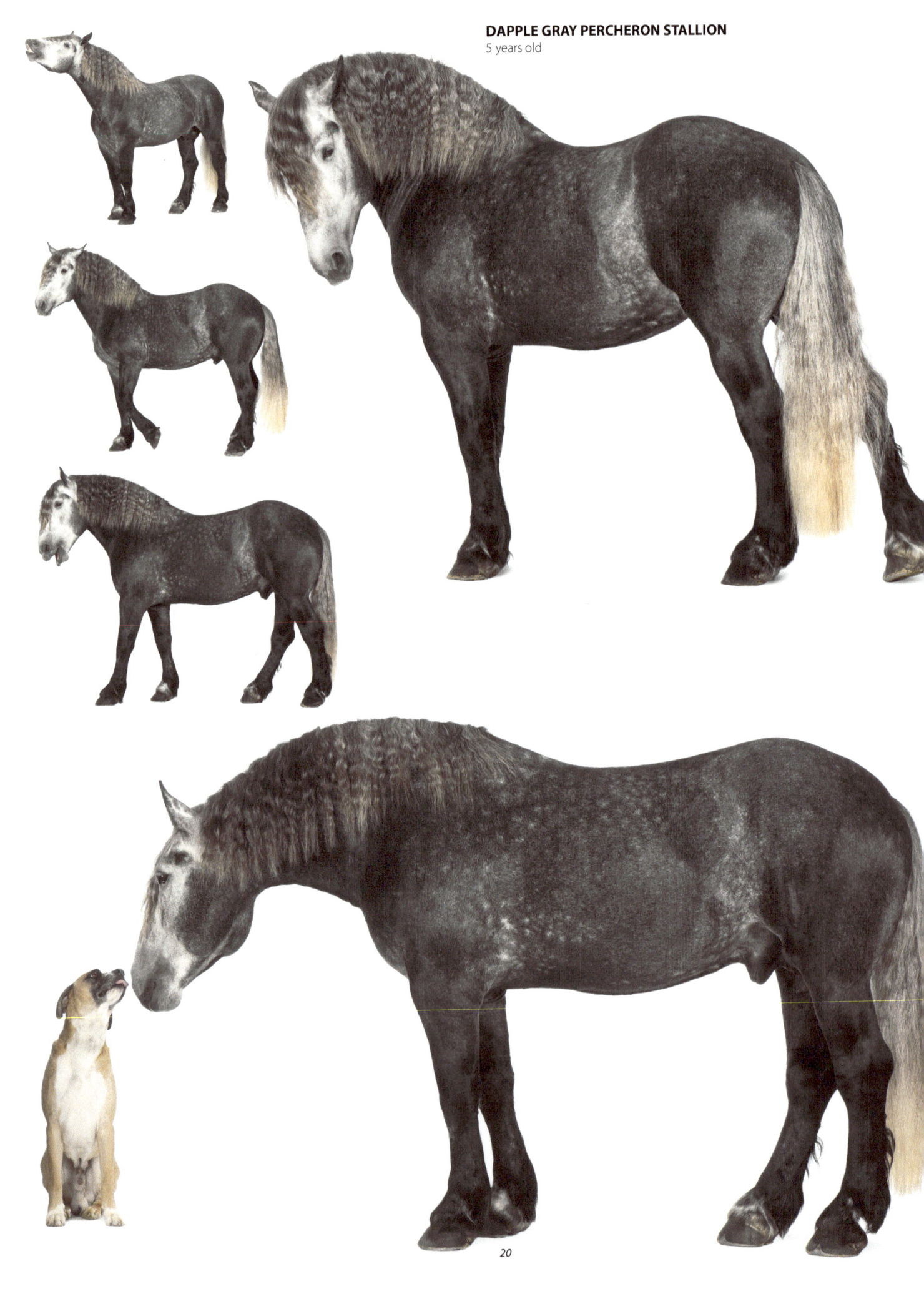

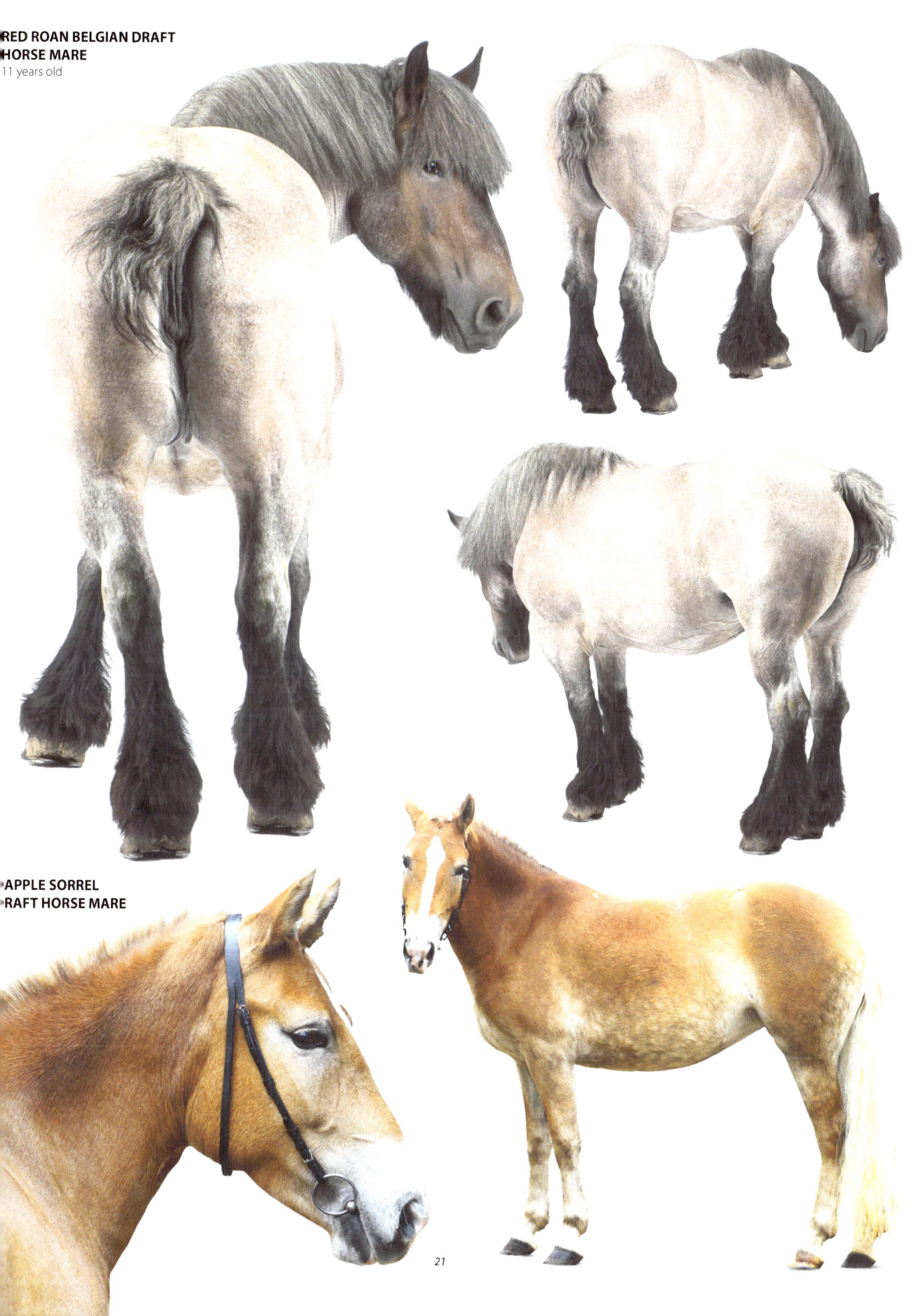

**RED ROAN BELGIAN DRAFT HORSE MARE**
11 years old

**APPLE SORREL DRAFT HORSE MARE**

21

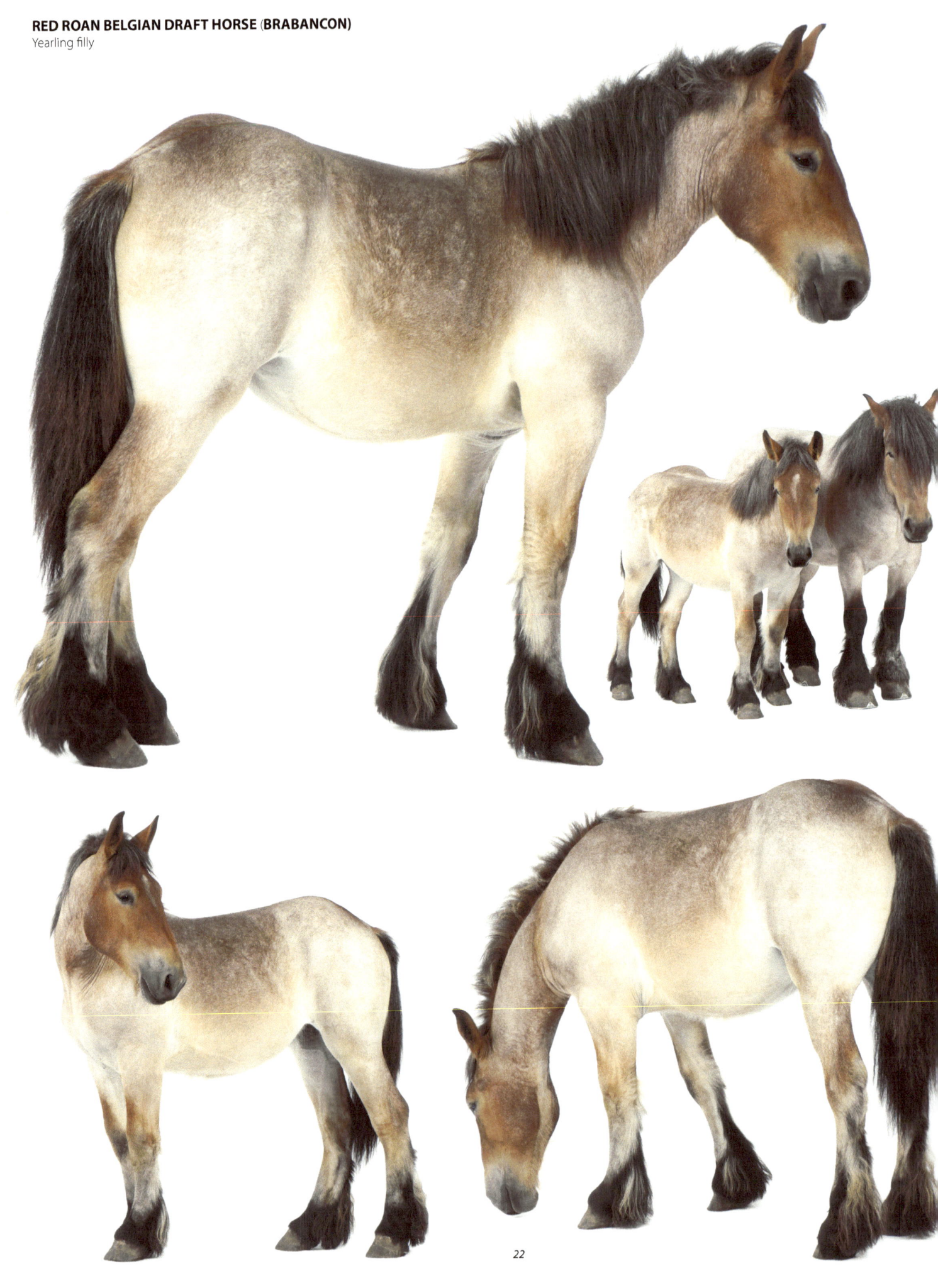

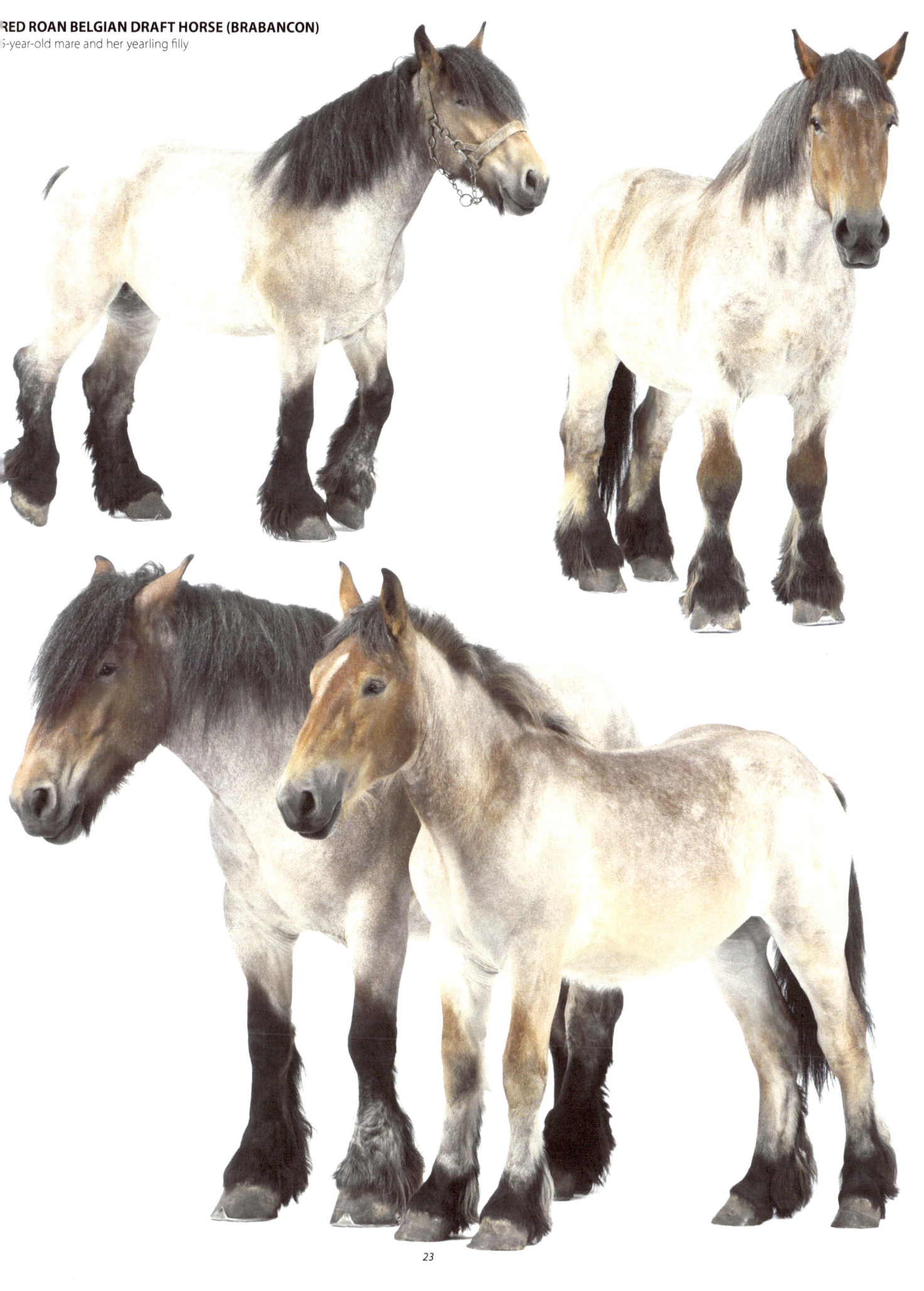

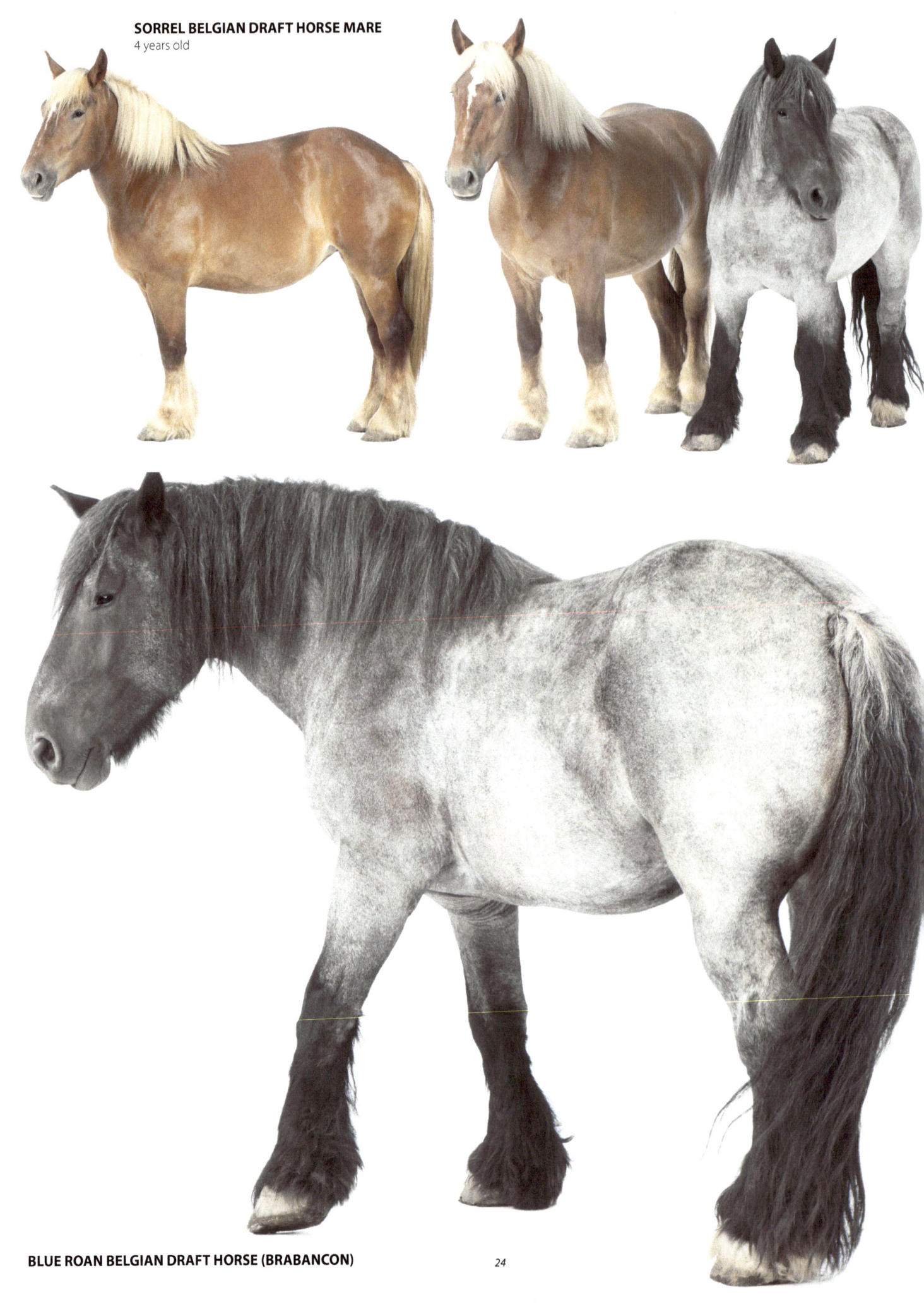

**SORREL BELGIAN DRAFT HORSE MARE**
4 years old

**BLUE ROAN BELGIAN DRAFT HORSE (BRABANCON)**

24

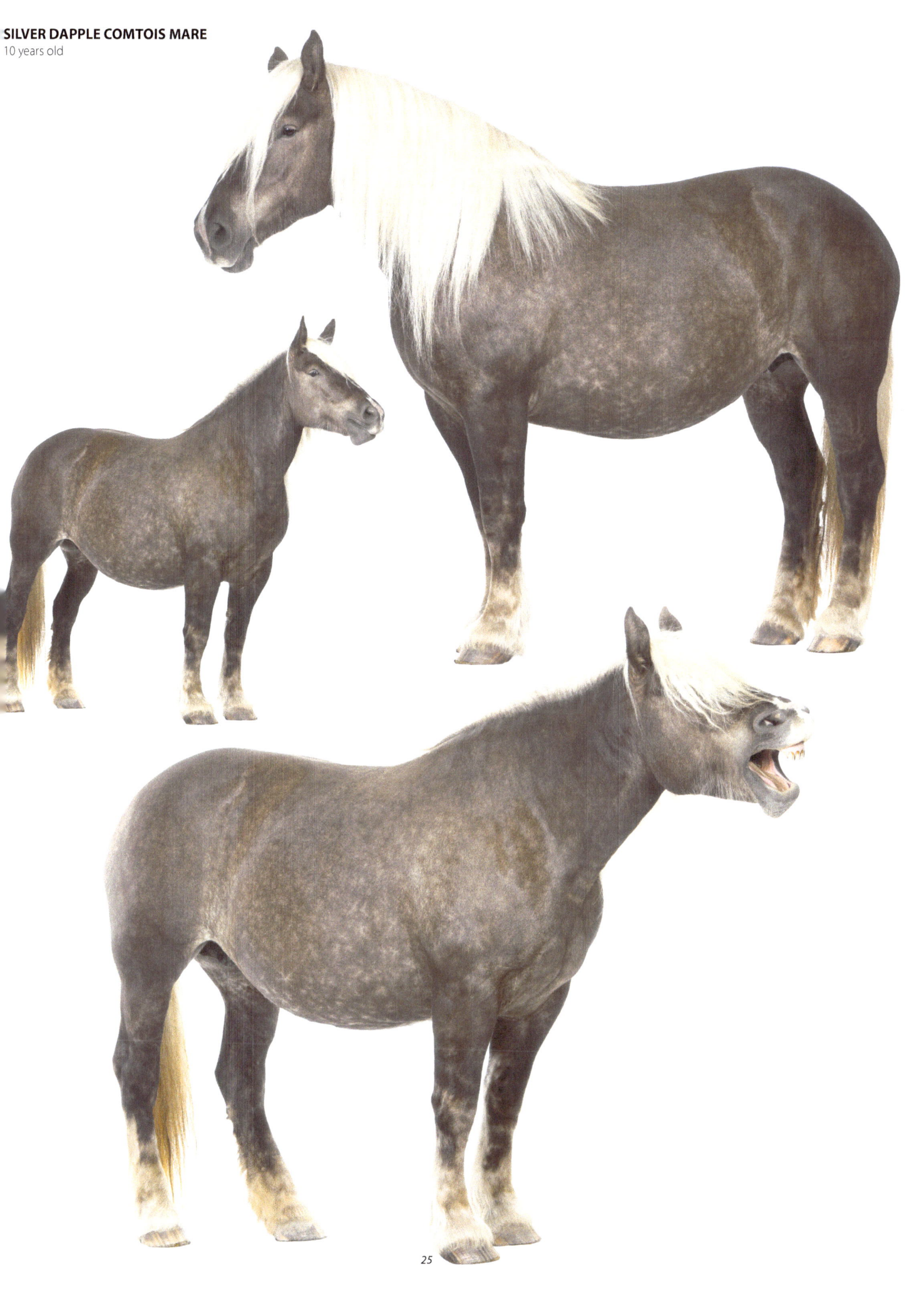

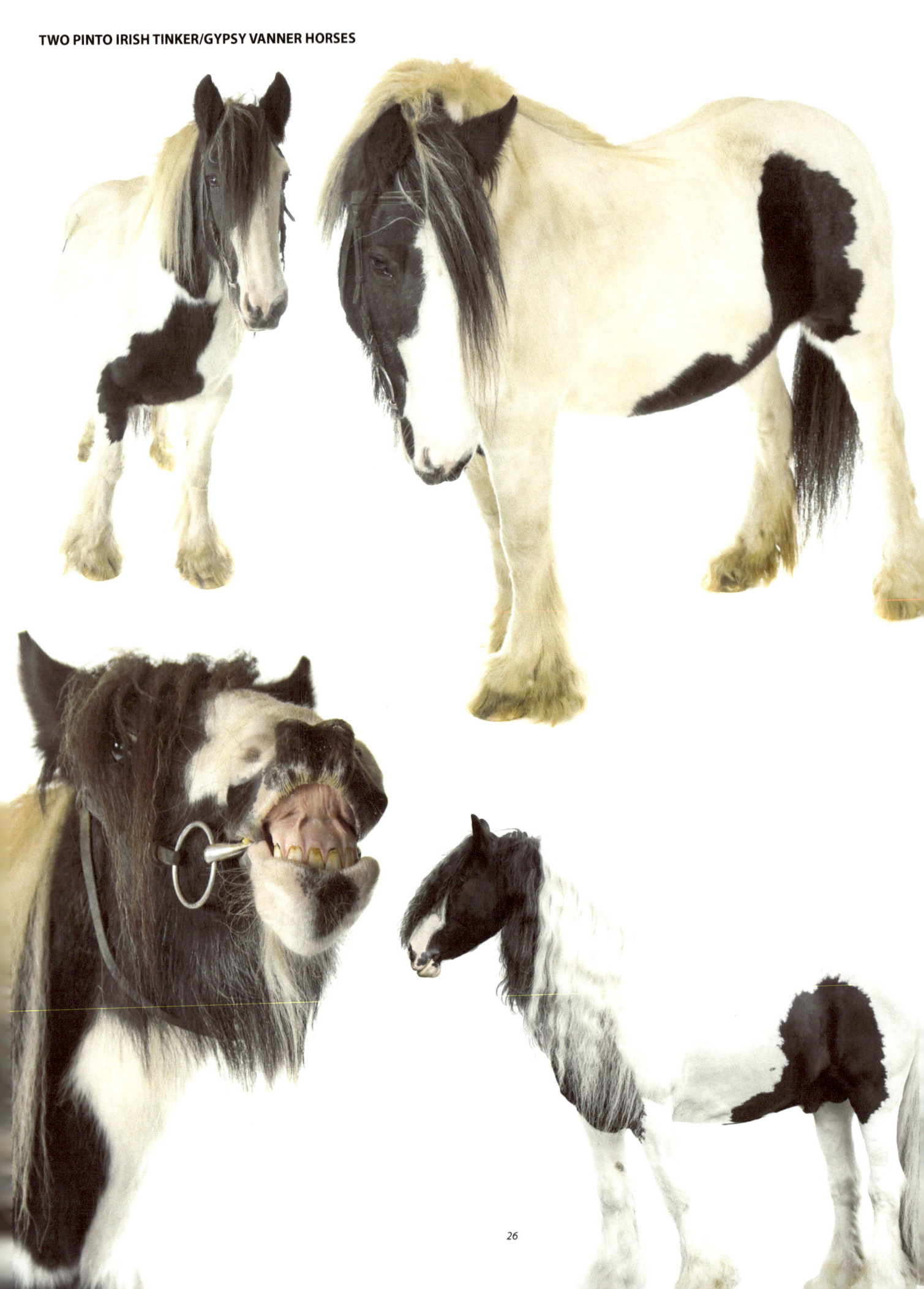

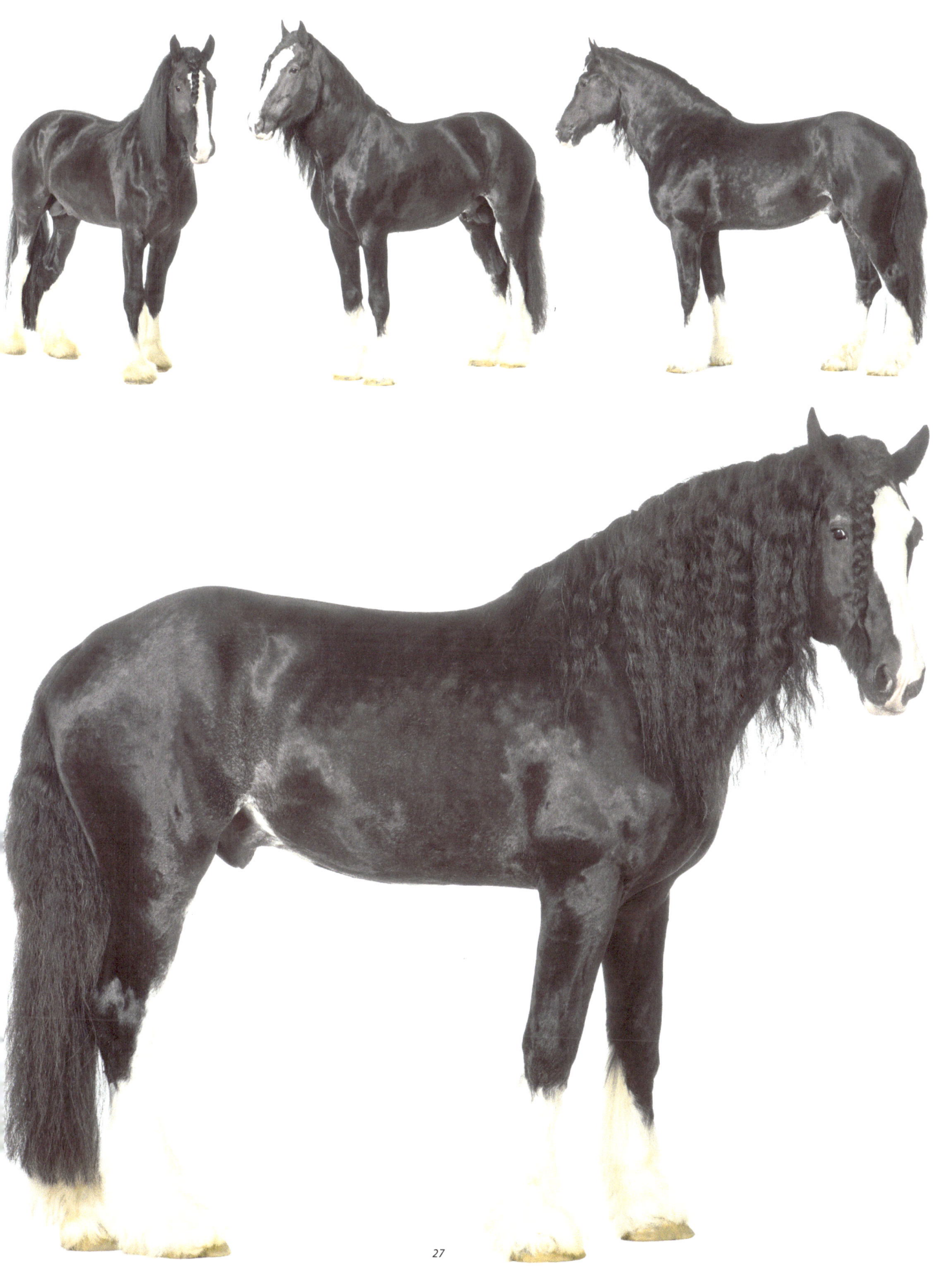

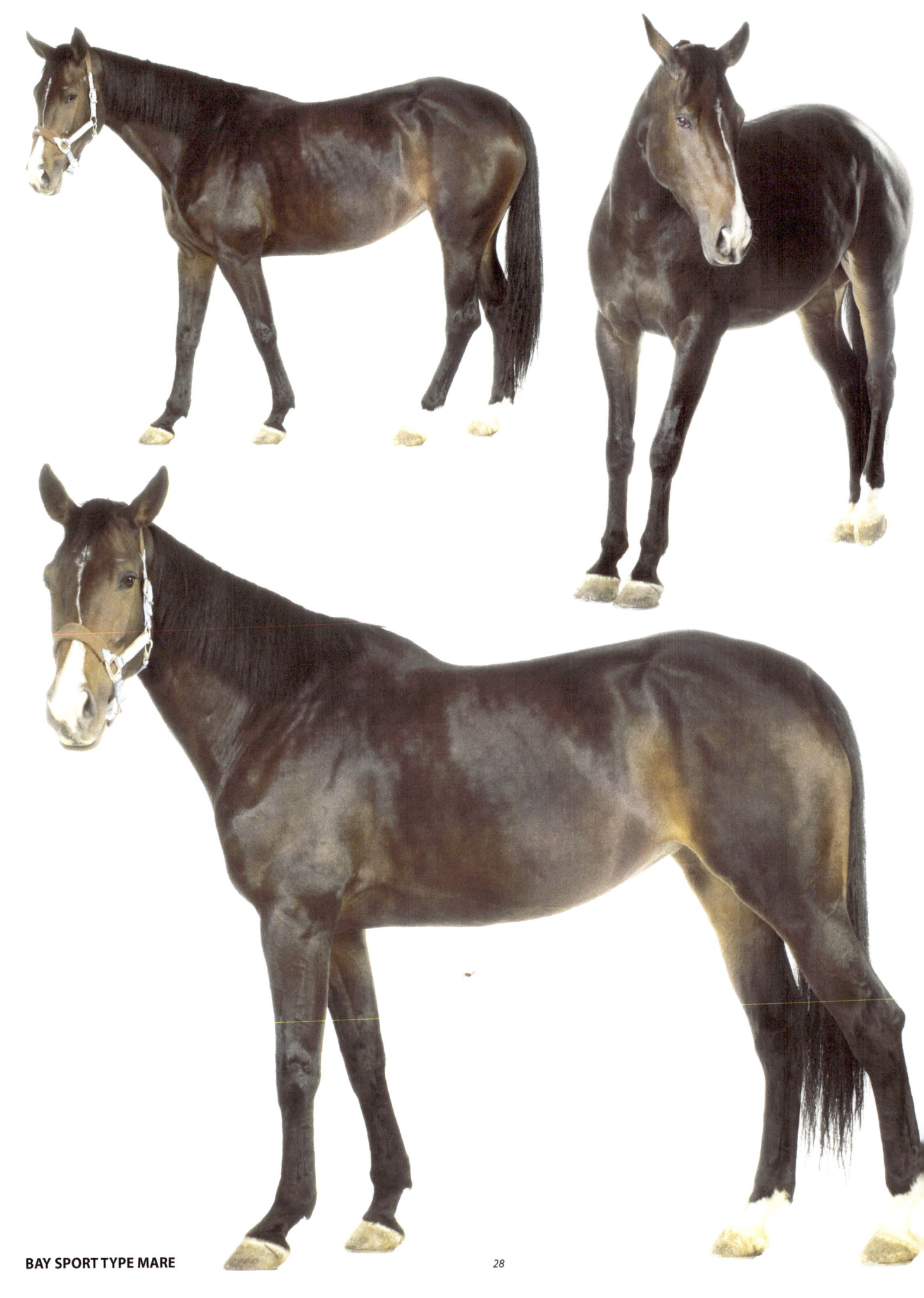

**BAY SPORT TYPE MARE**

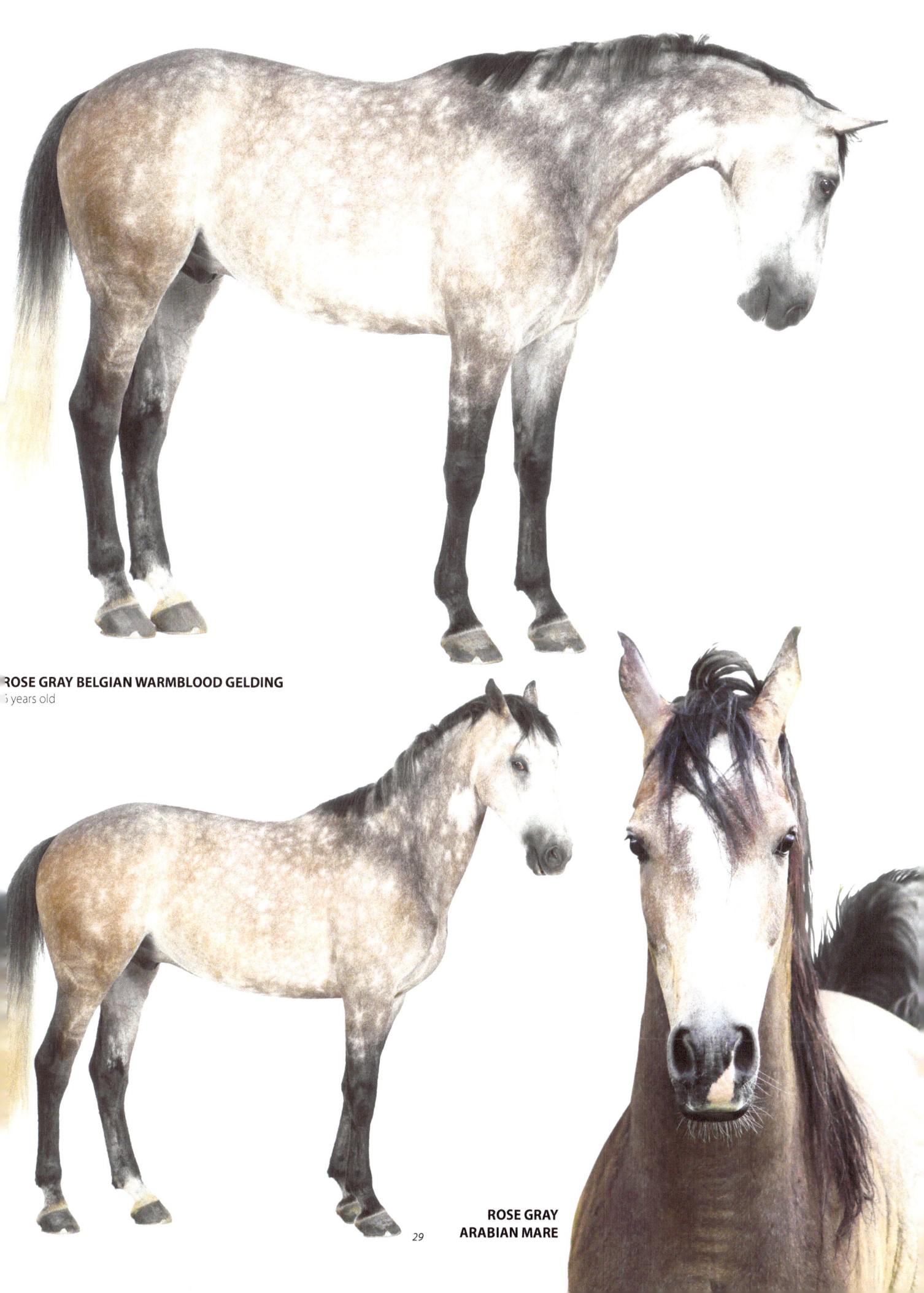

**ROSE GRAY BELGIAN WARMBLOOD GELDING**
5 years old

**ROSE GRAY
ARABIAN MARE**

29

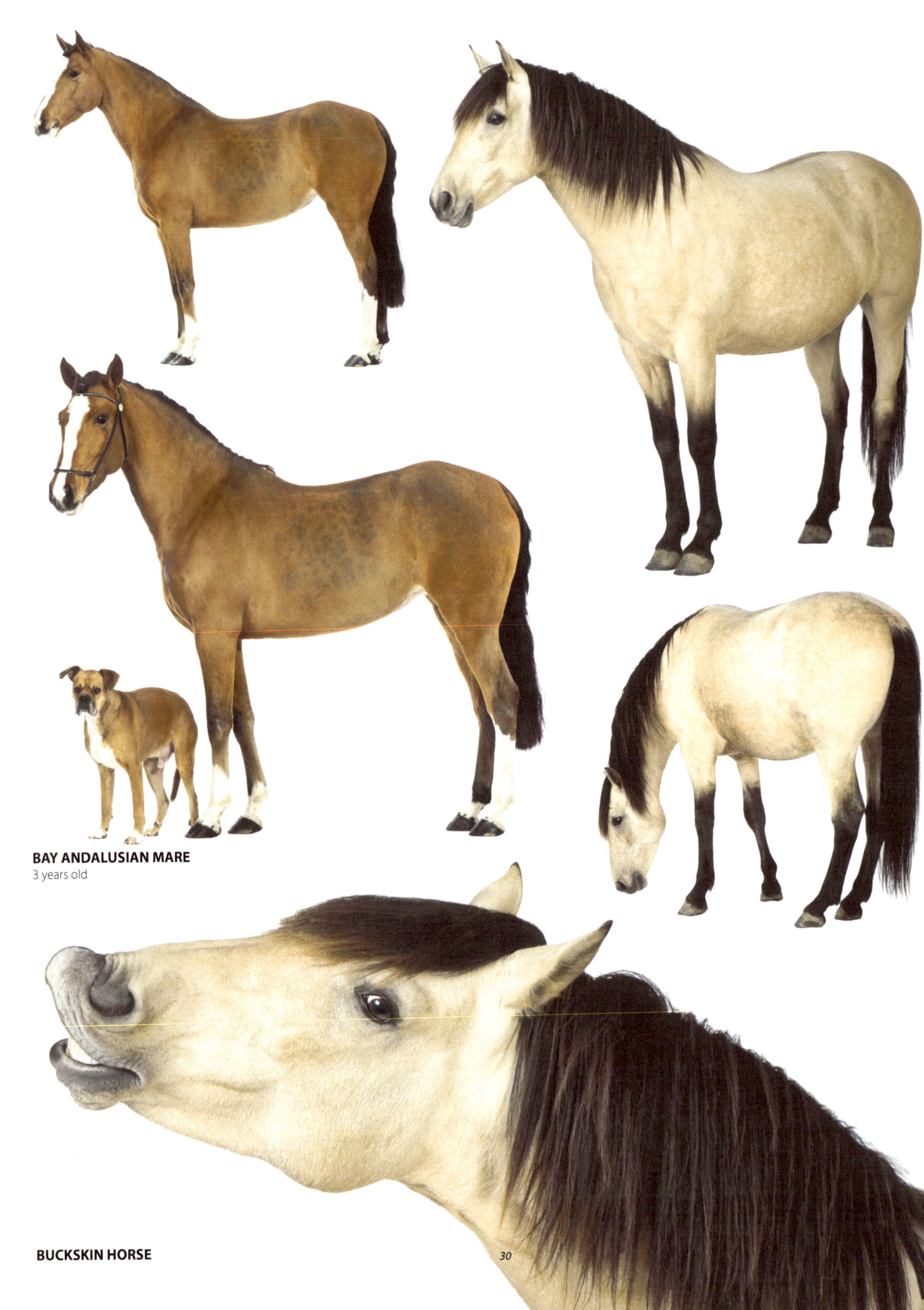

**BAY ANDALUSIAN MARE**
3 years old

**BUCKSKIN HORSE**

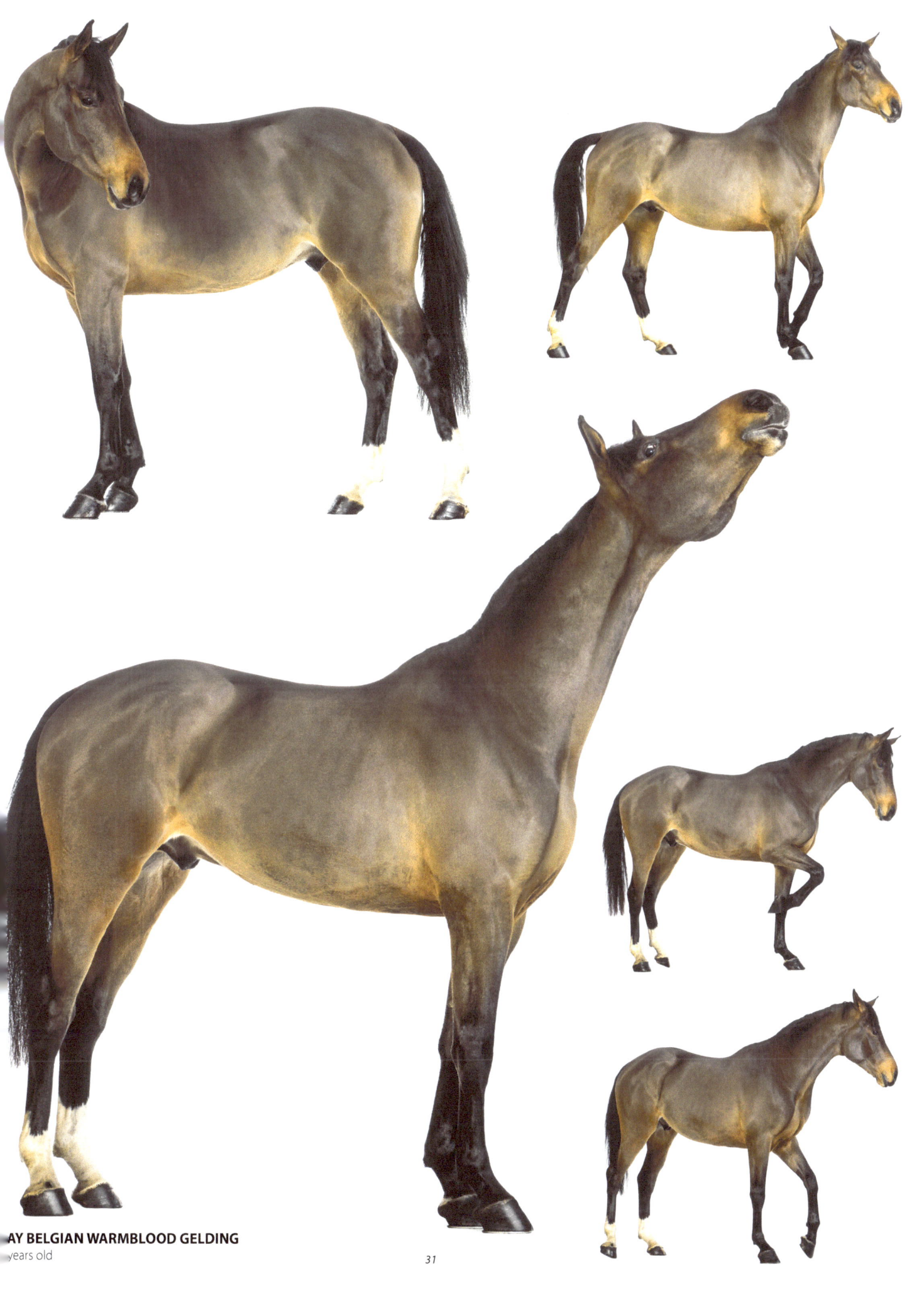

**AY BELGIAN WARMBLOOD GELDING**
years old

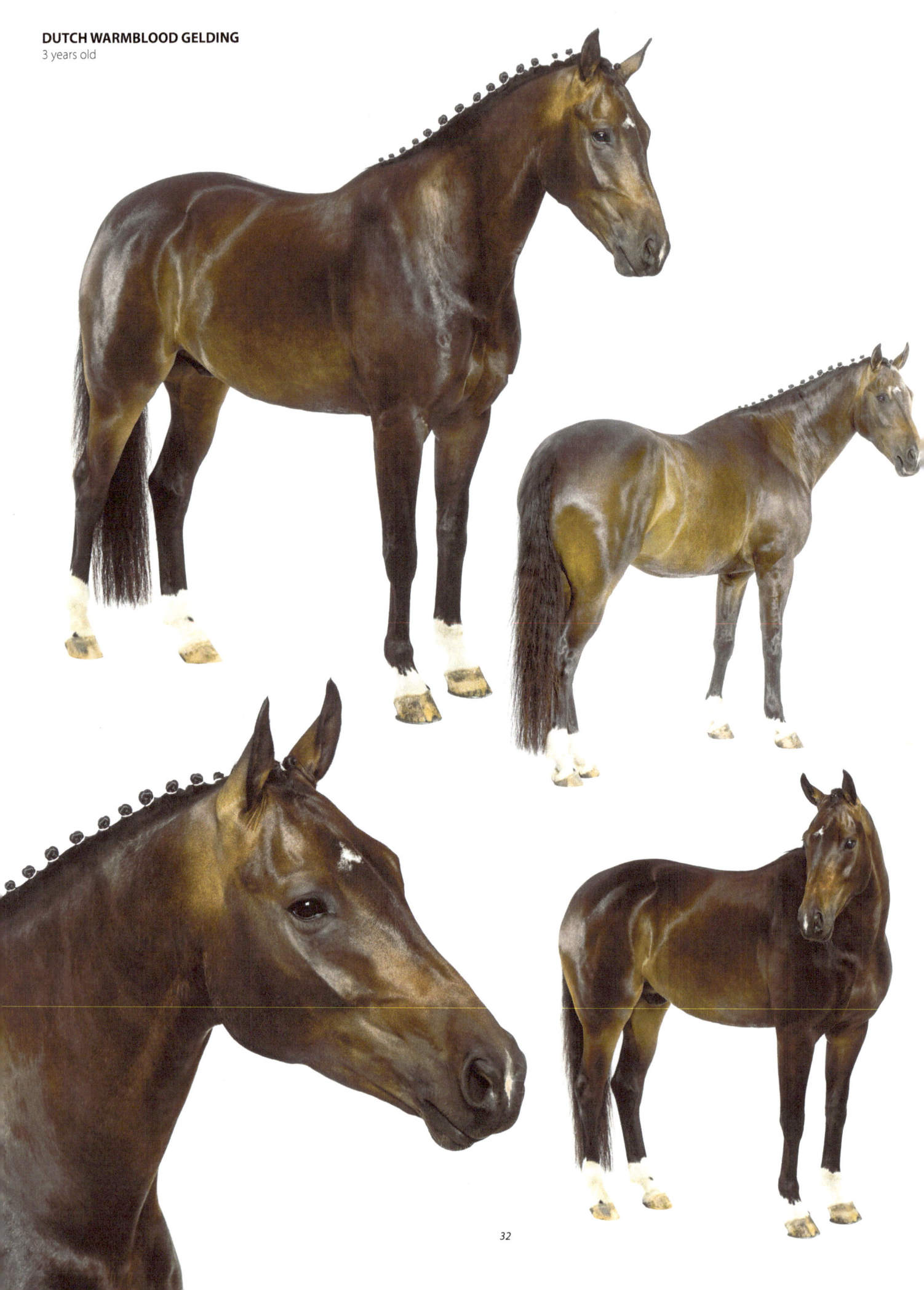

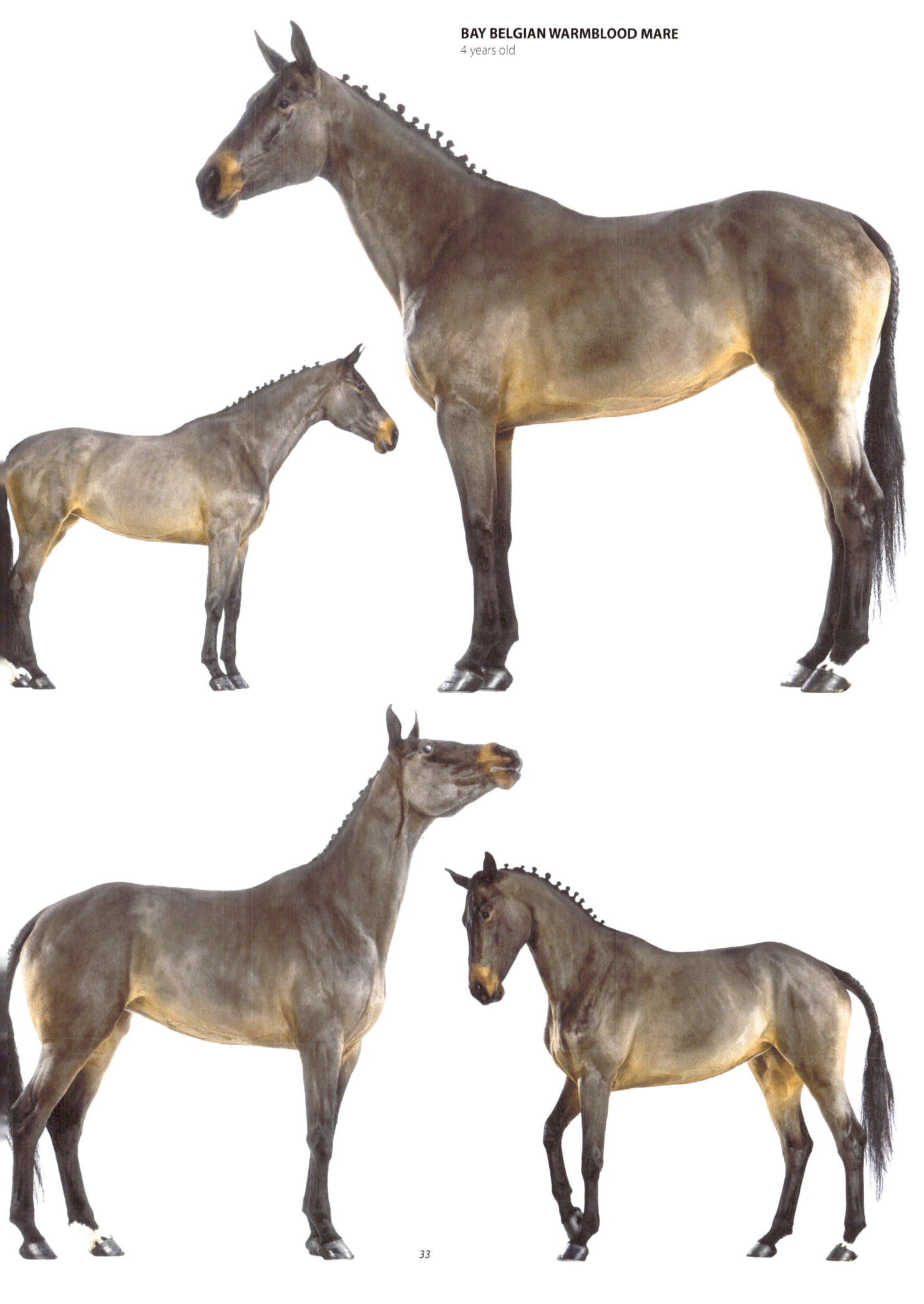

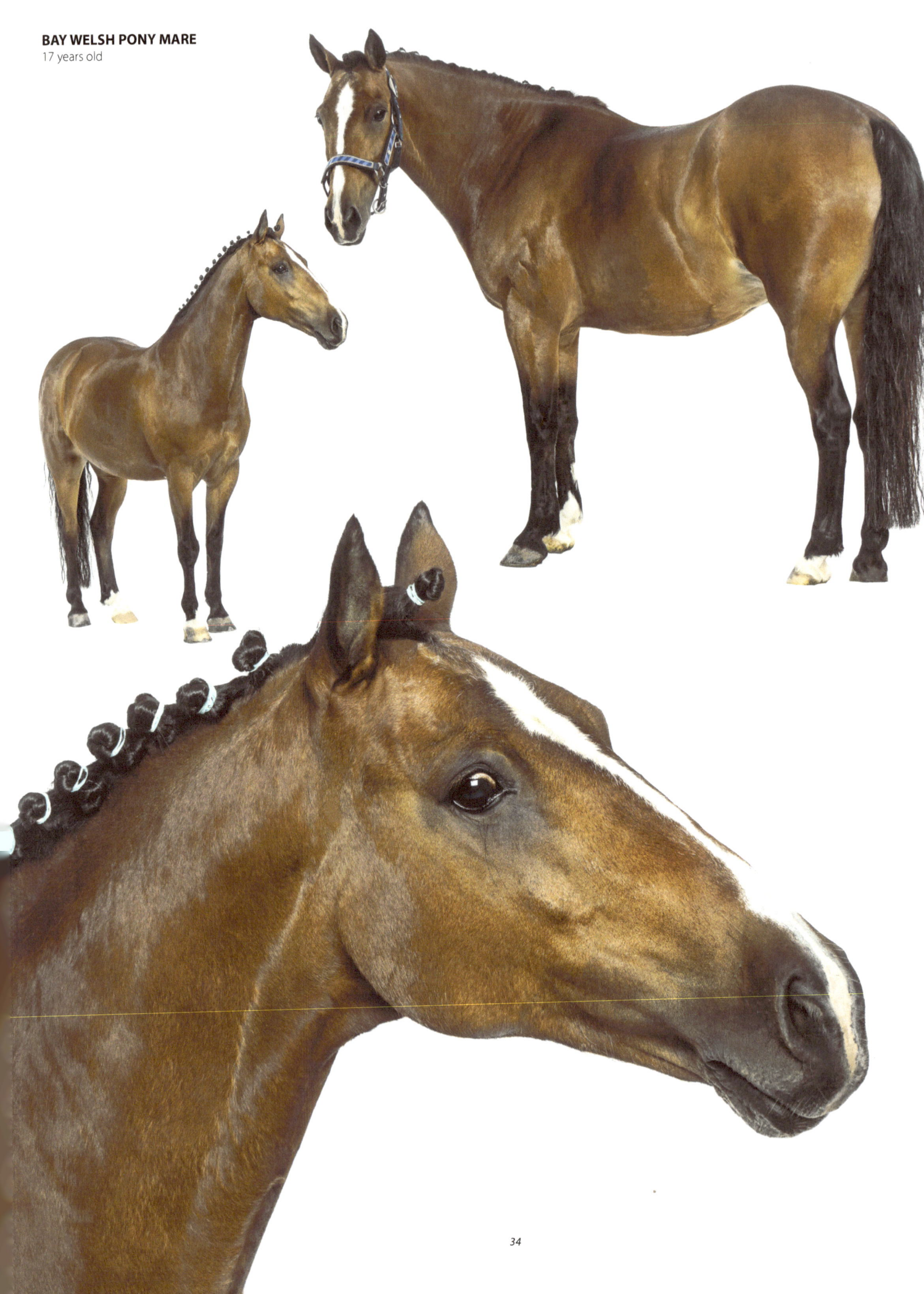

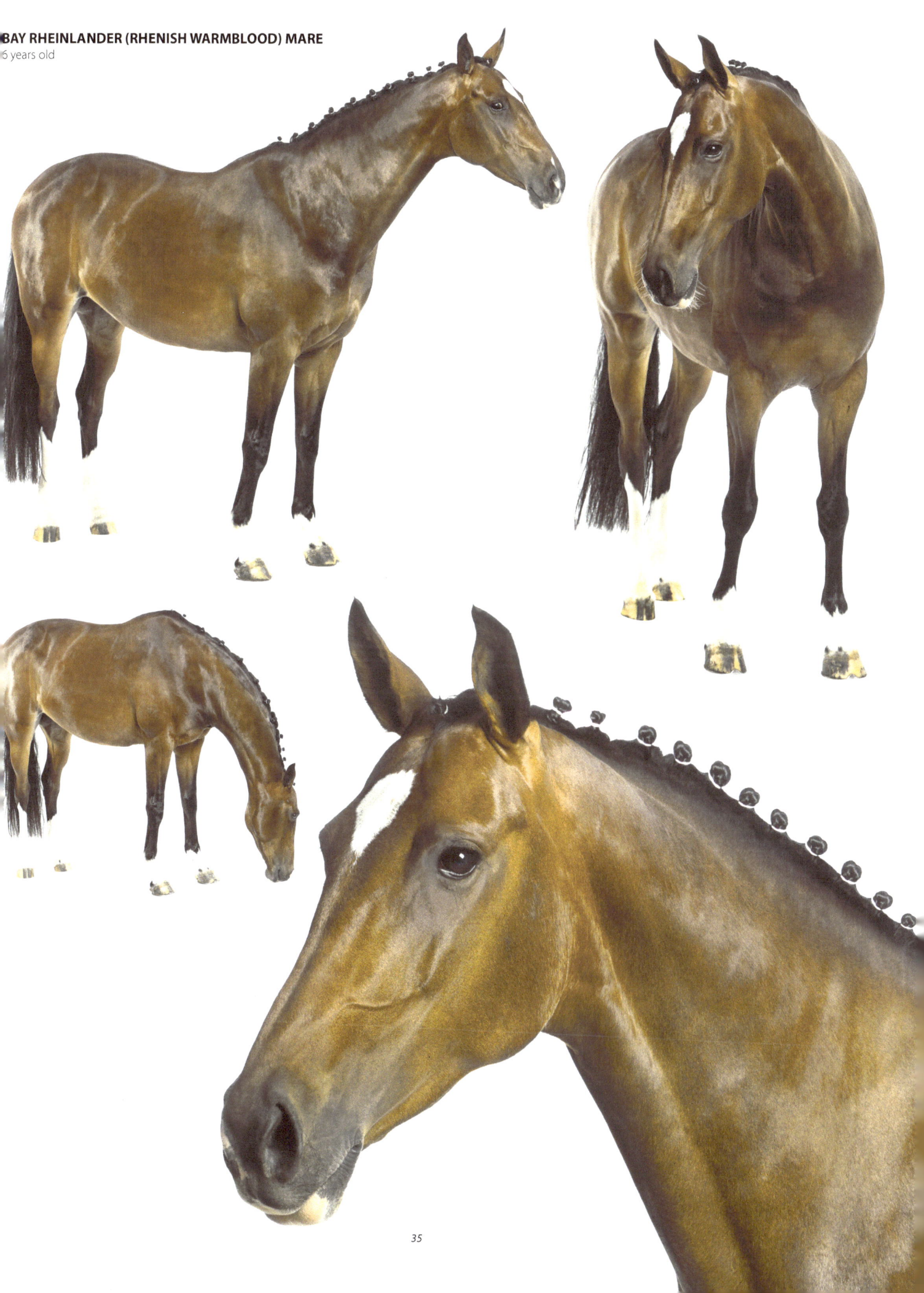

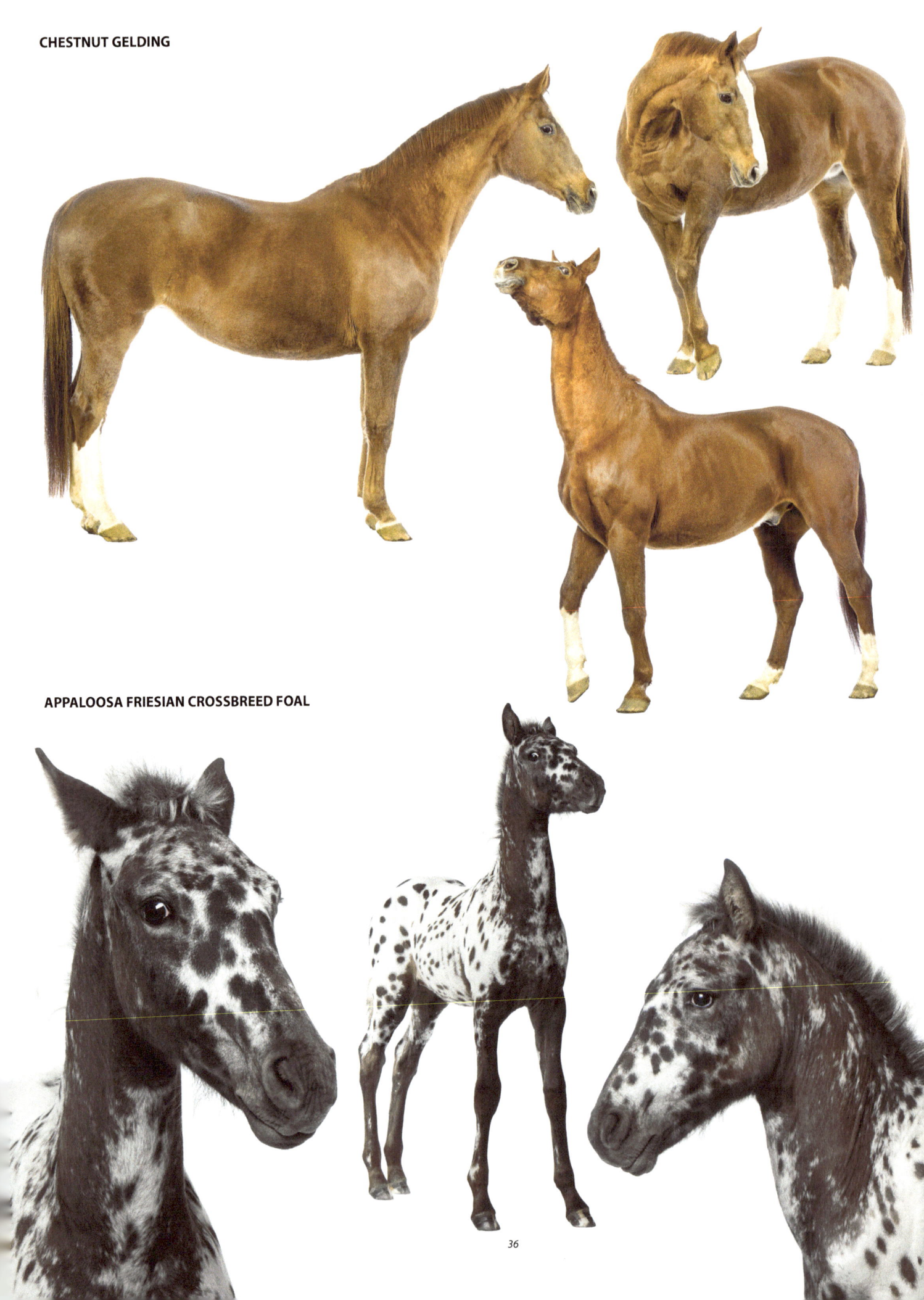

**CHESTNUT GELDING**

**APPALOOSA FRIESIAN CROSSBREED FOAL**

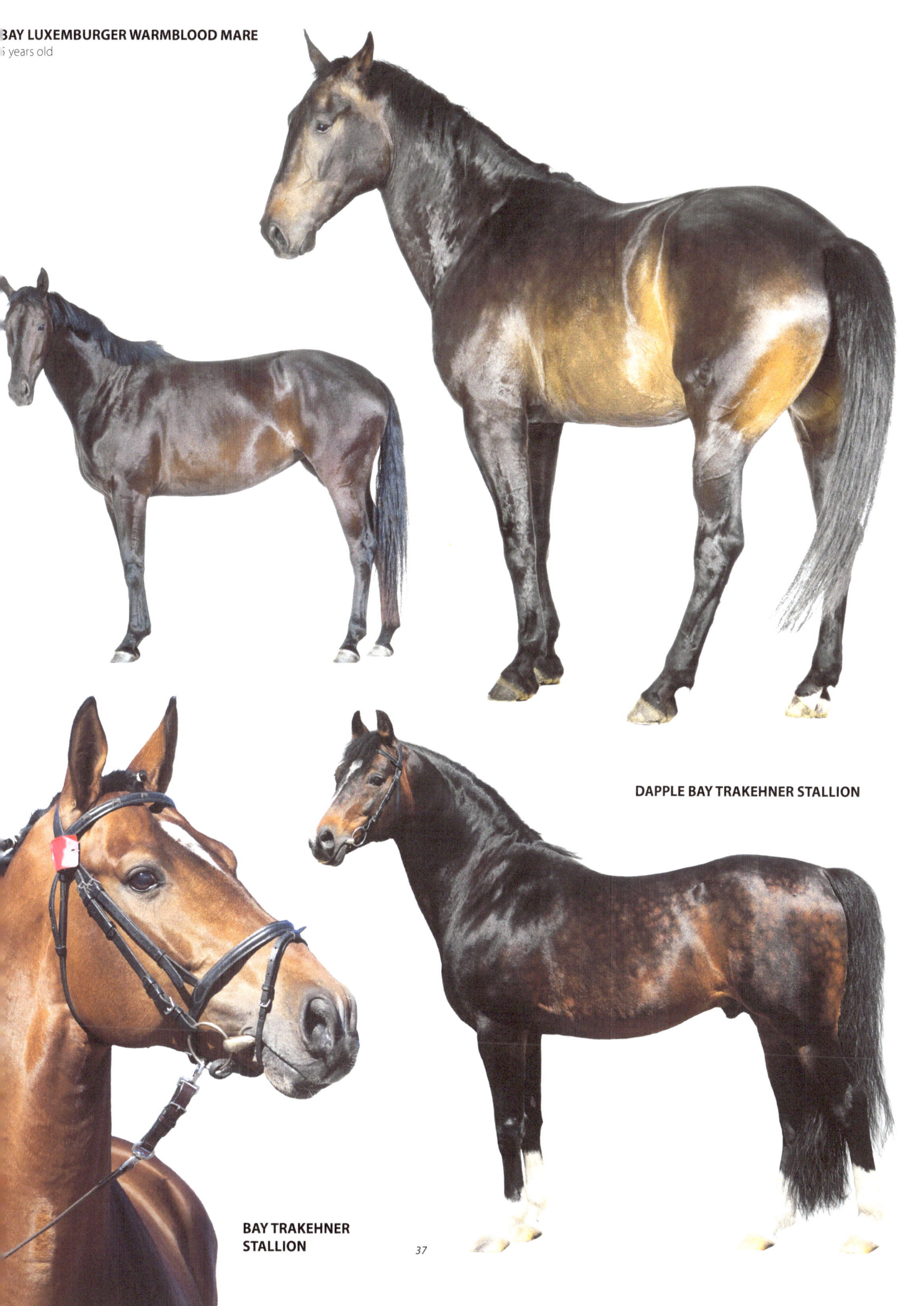

**BAY LUXEMBURGER WARMBLOOD MARE**
5 years old

**DAPPLE BAY TRAKEHNER STALLION**

**BAY TRAKEHNER STALLION**

37

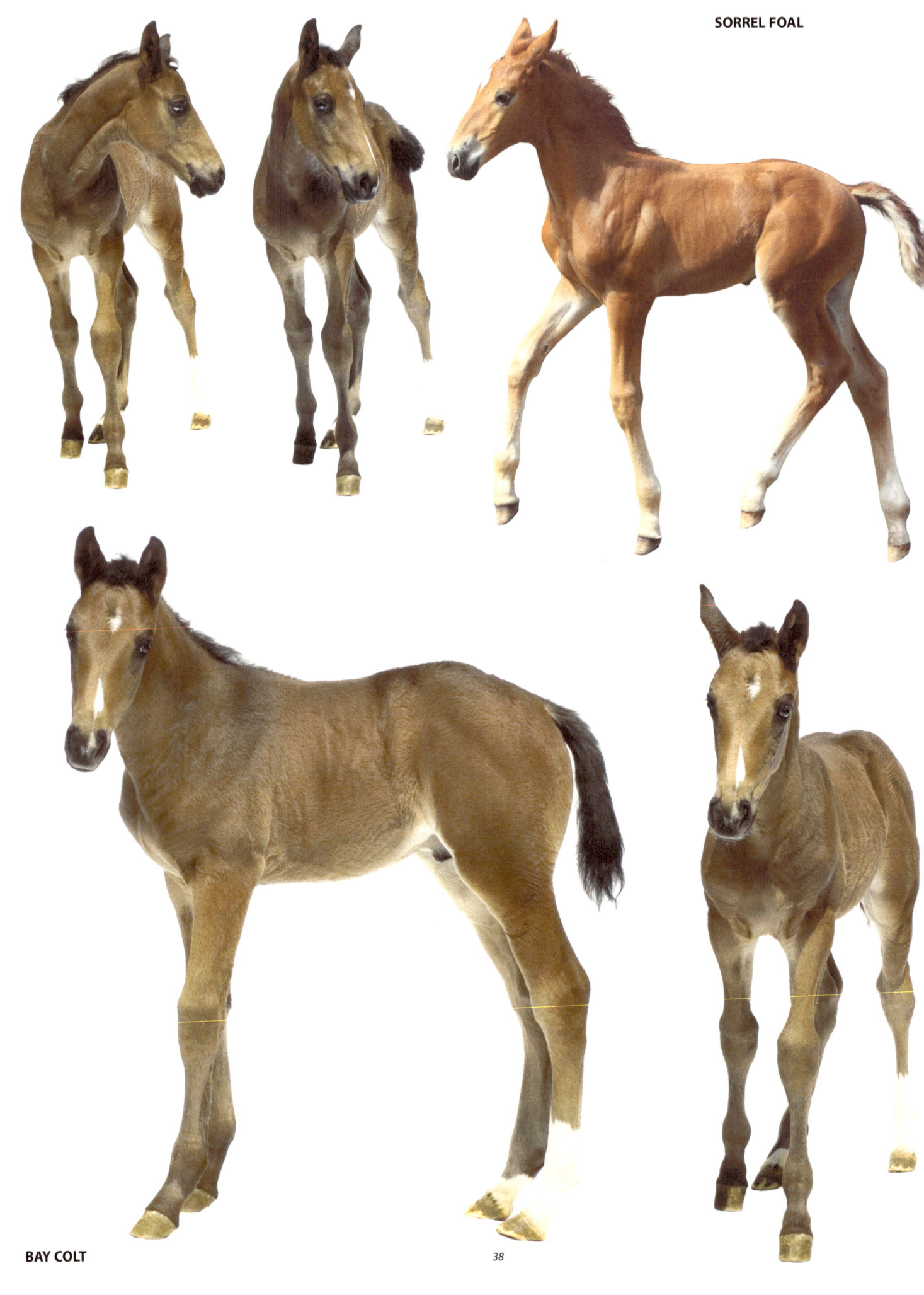

BAY COLT

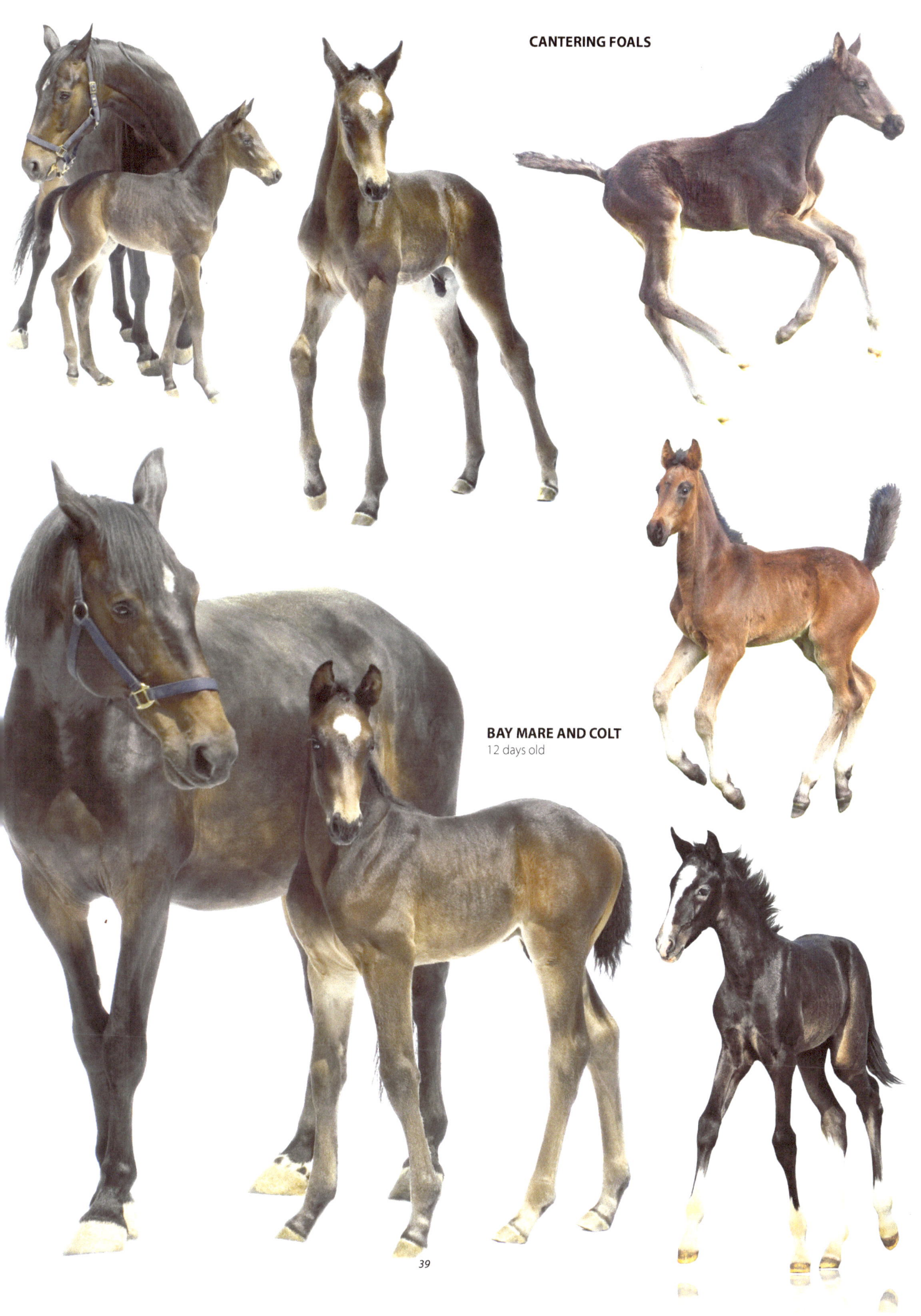

BAY MARE AND COLT
12 days old

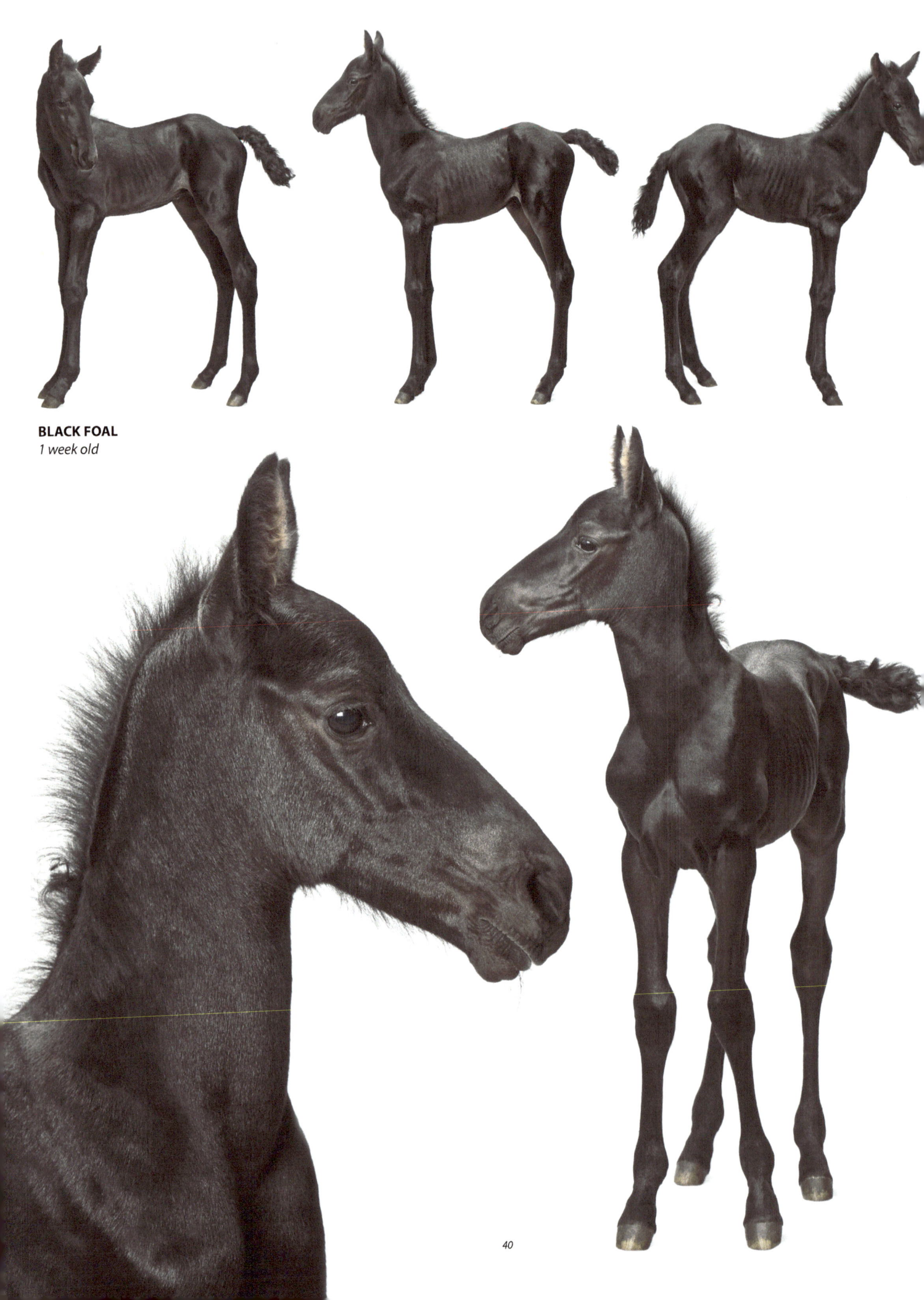

**BLACK FOAL**
*1 week old*

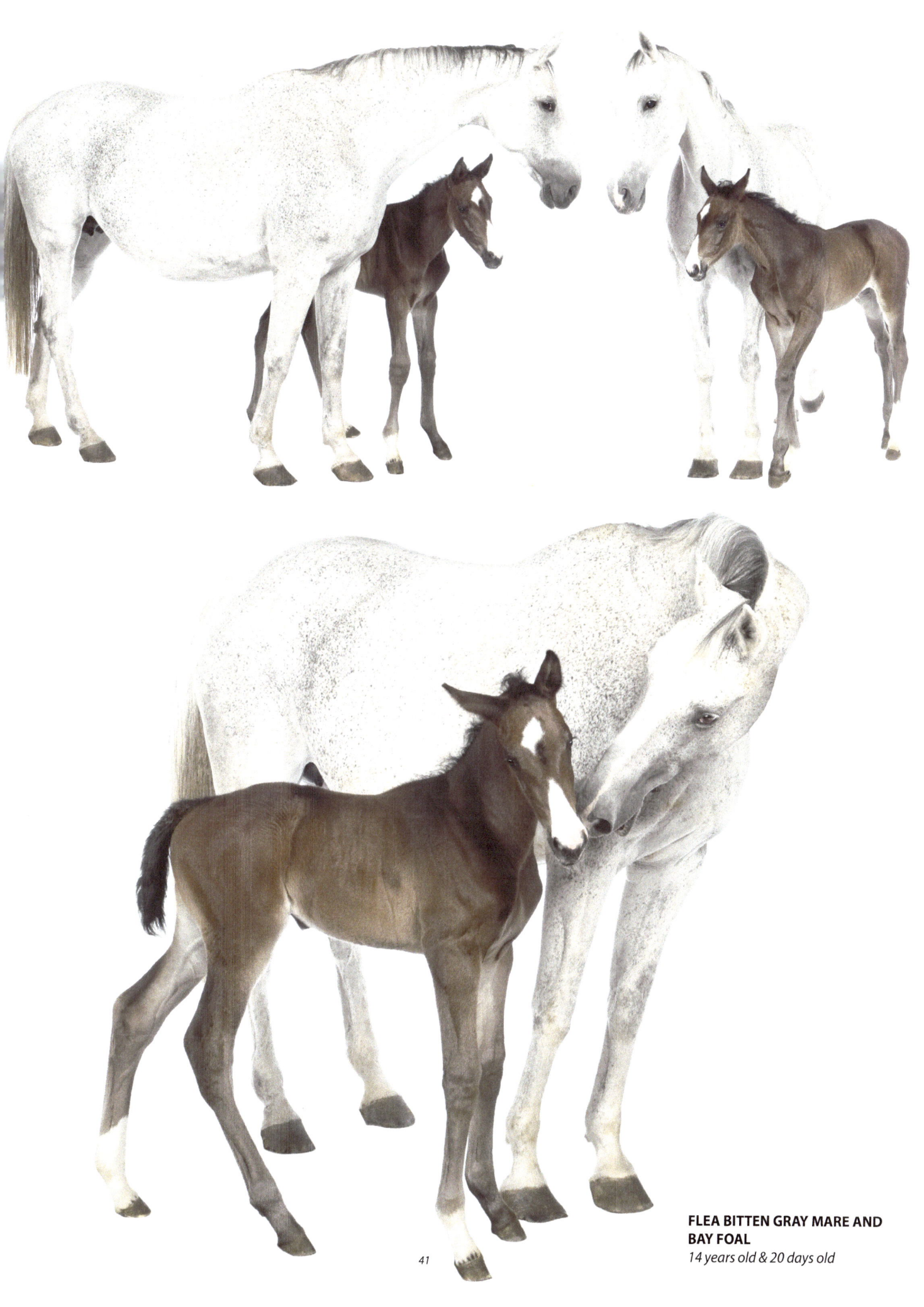

**FLEA BITTEN GRAY MARE AND BAY FOAL**
*14 years old & 20 days old*

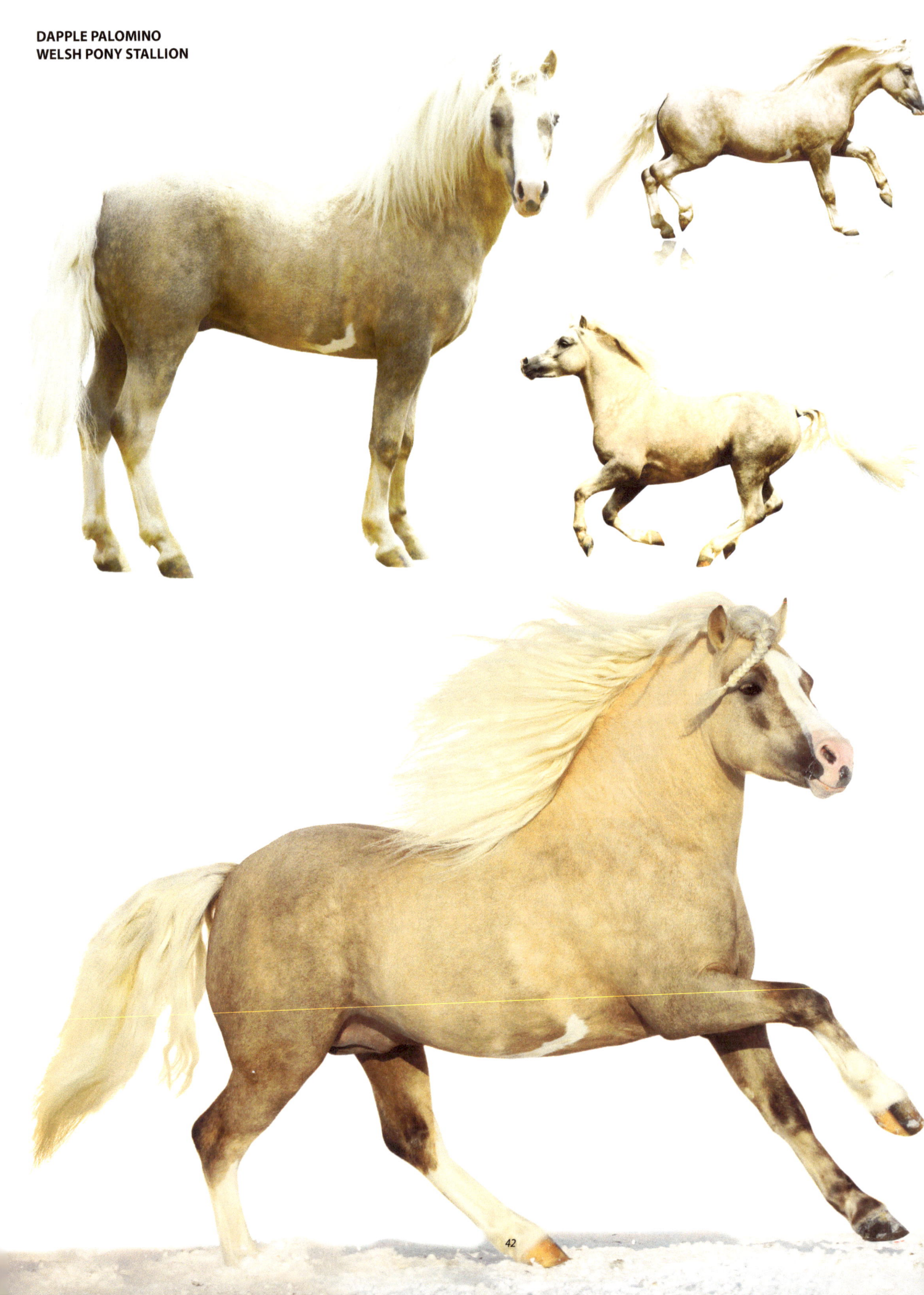

**PALOMINO WELSH PONY MARE AND FOAL**

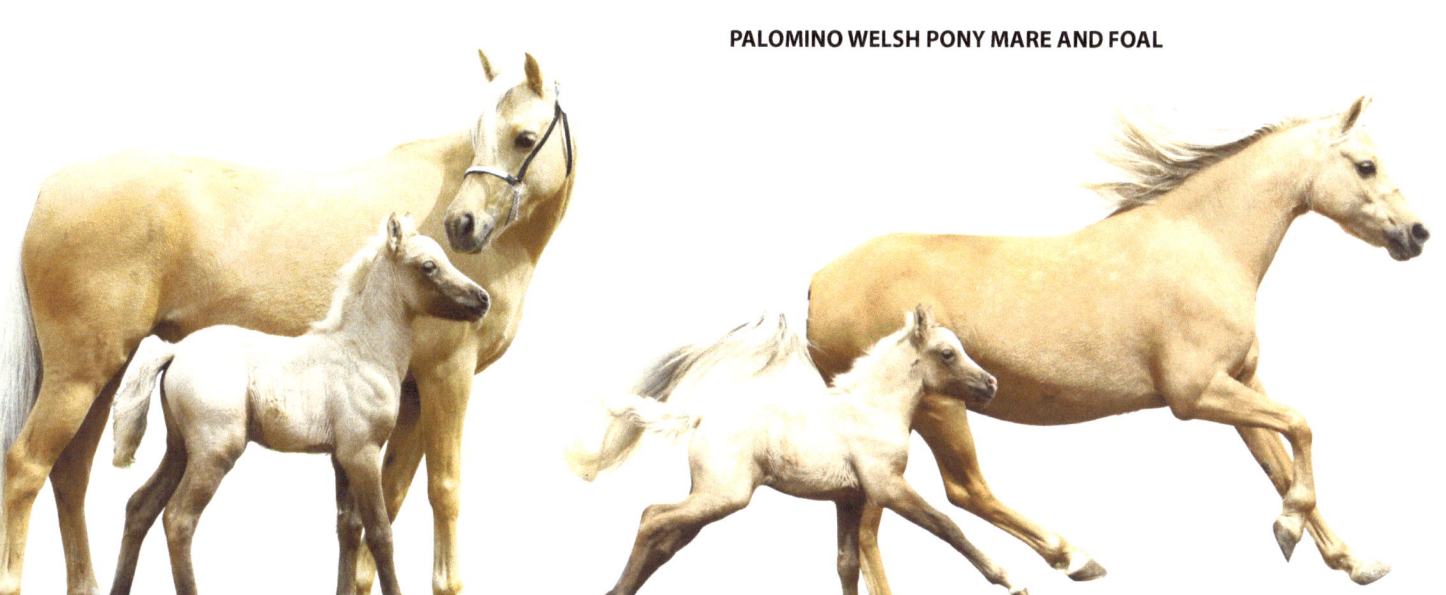

**HALFLINGER PONY MARE**
23 years old

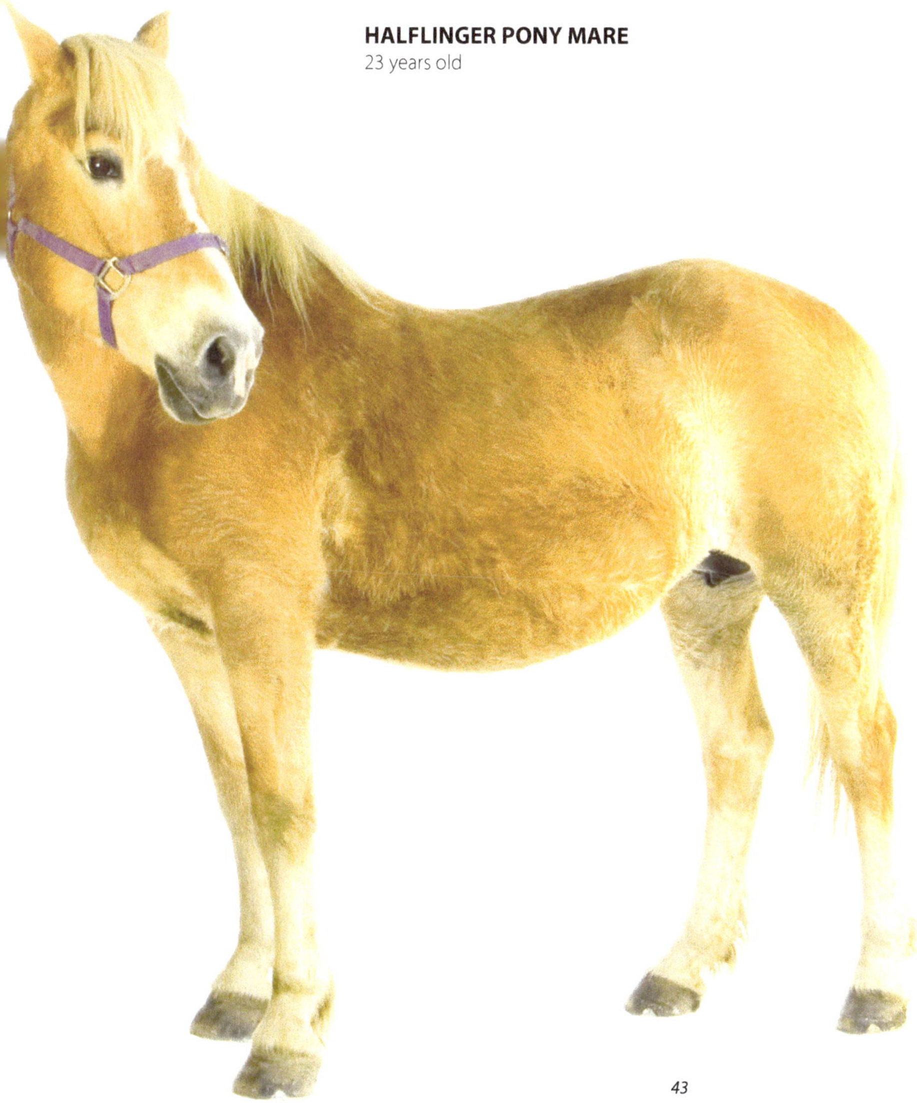

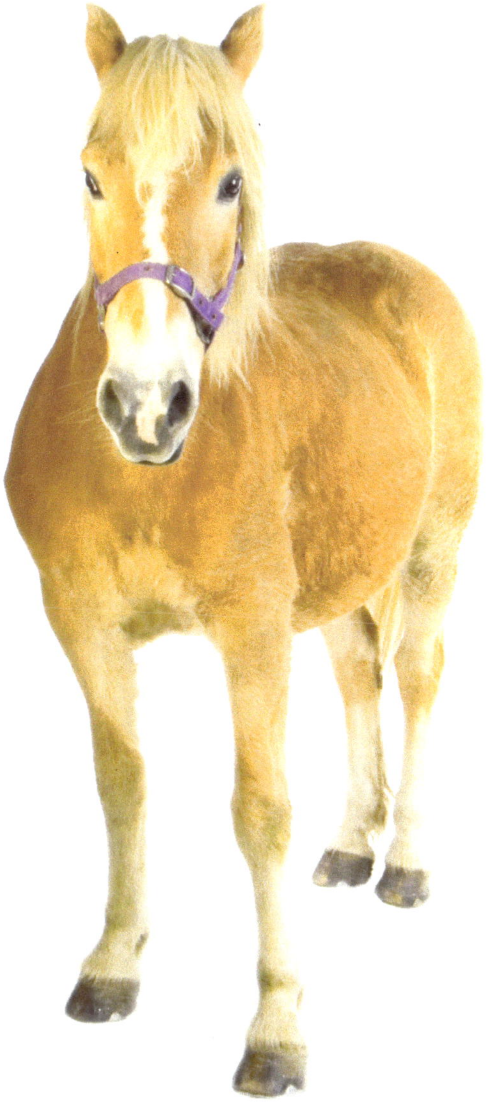

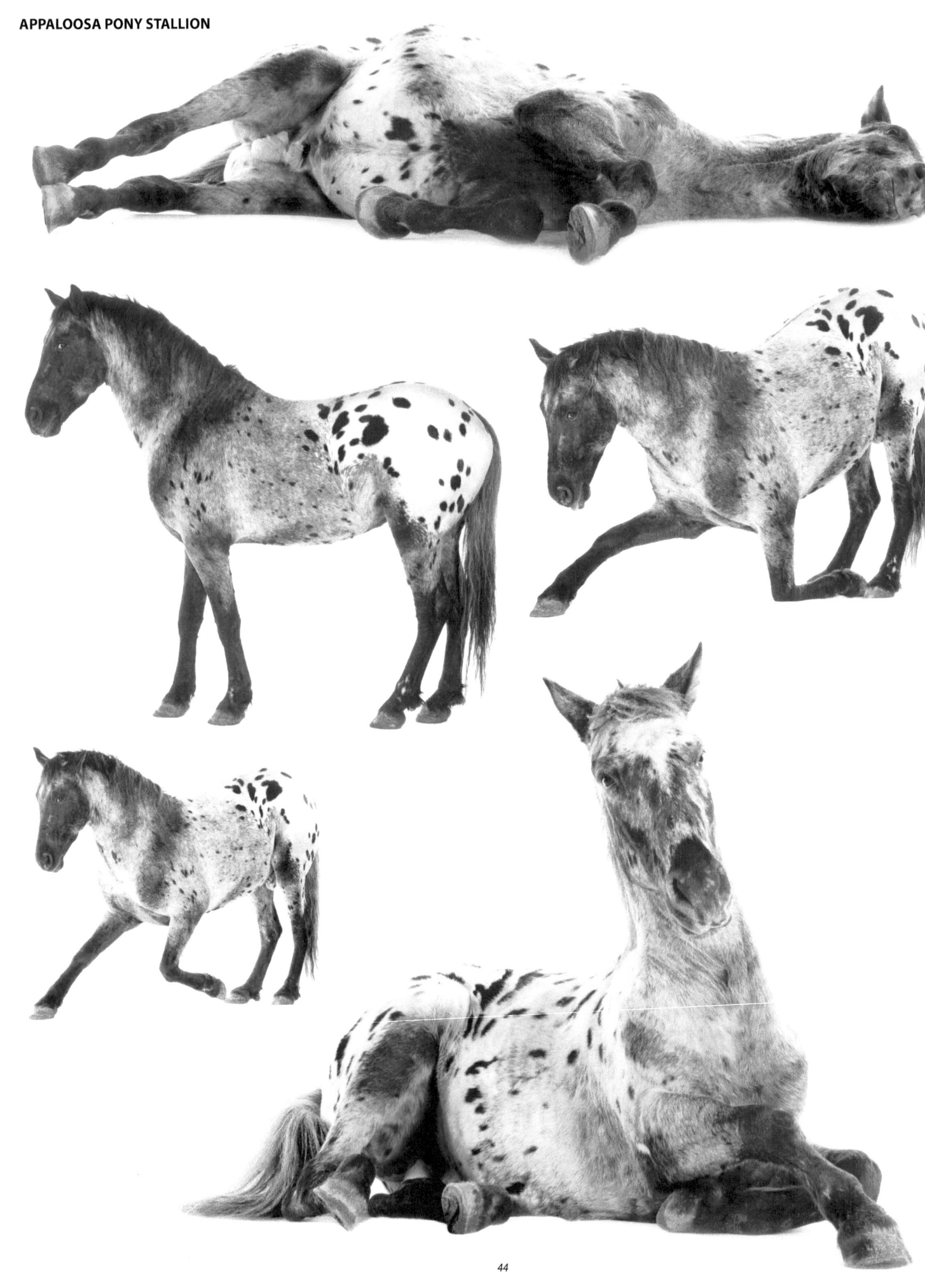

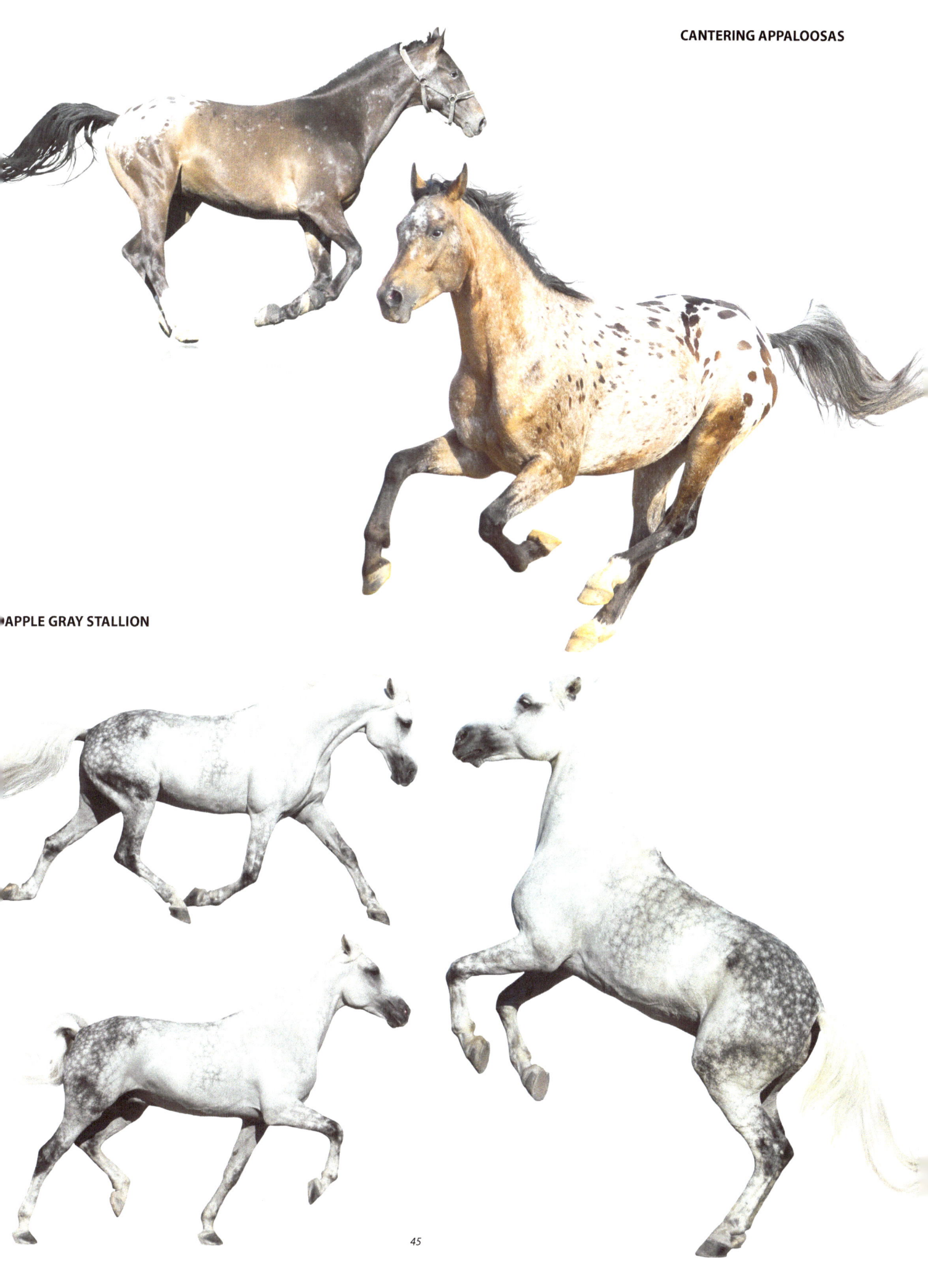

APPLE GRAY STALLION

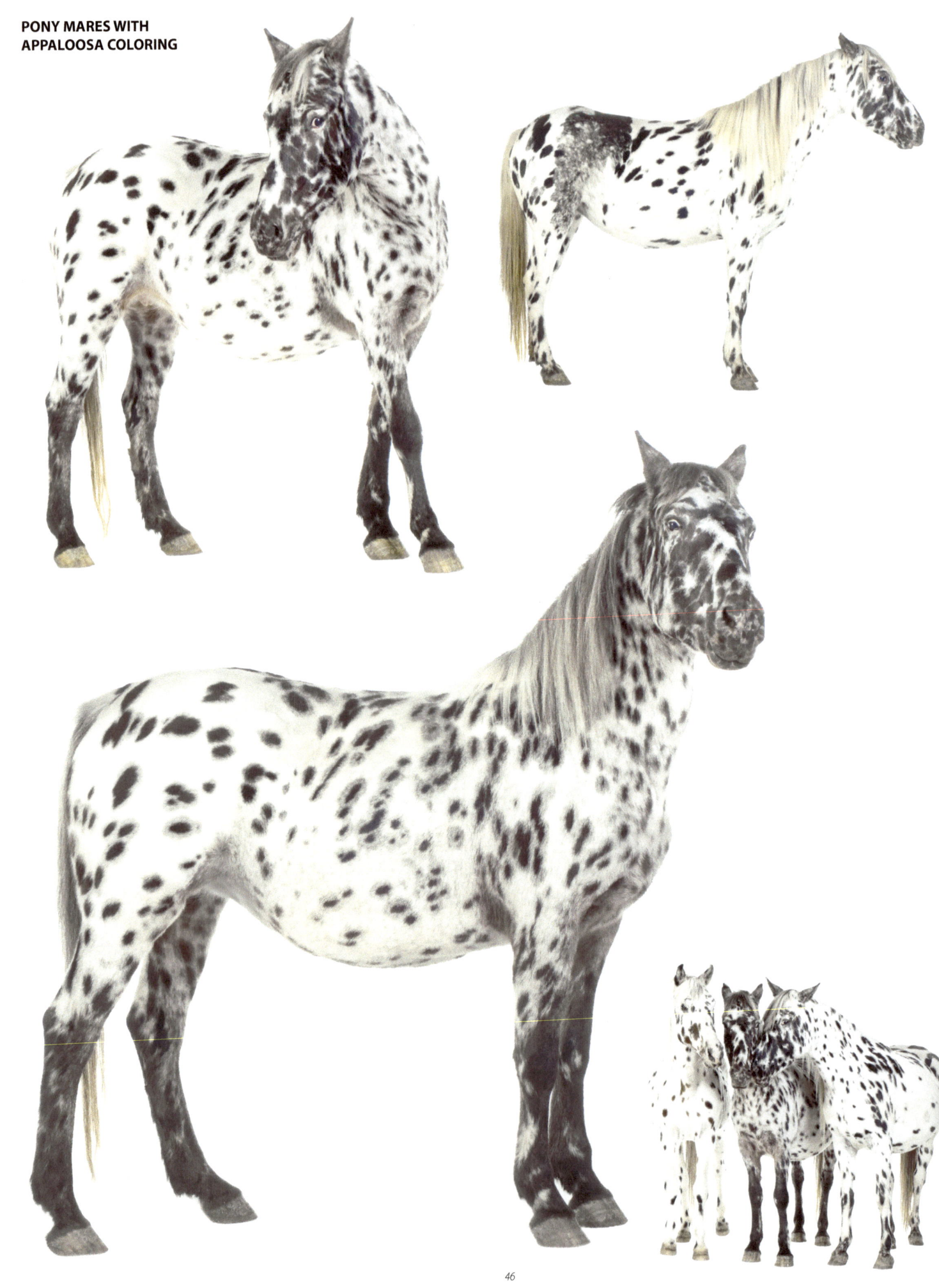

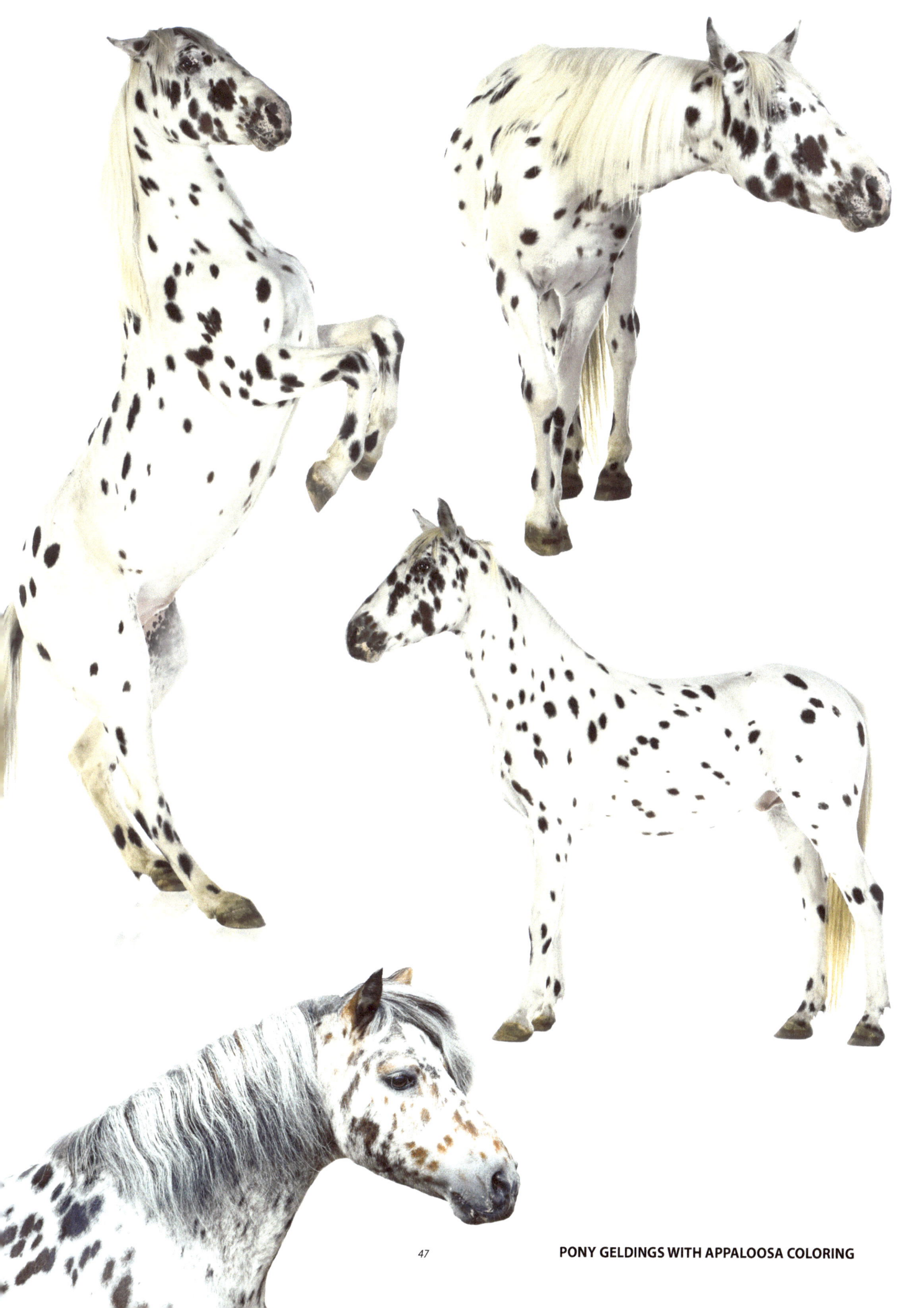

47　**PONY GELDINGS WITH APPALOOSA COLORING**

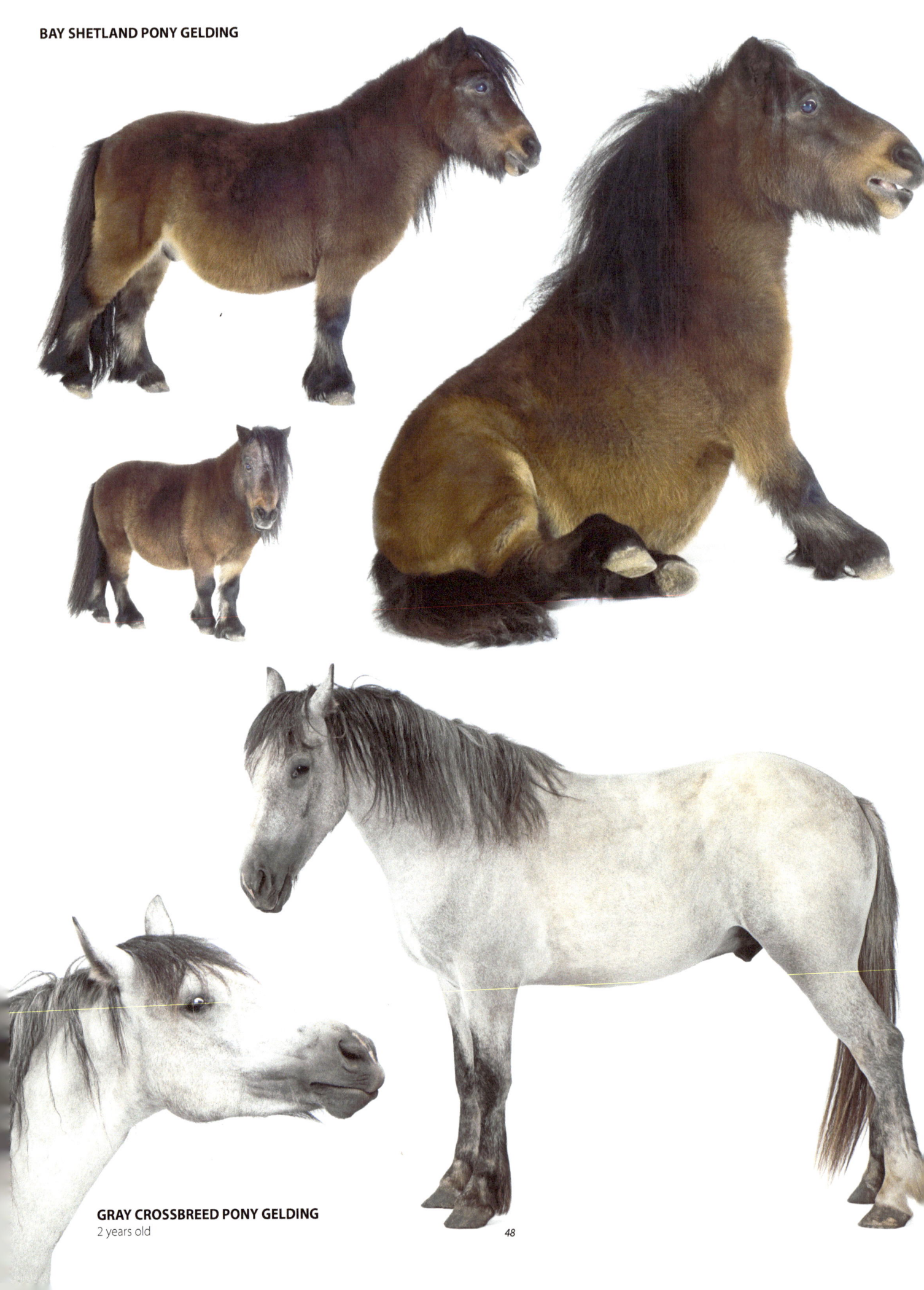

**BAY SHETLAND PONY GELDING**

**GRAY CROSSBREED PONY GELDING**
2 years old

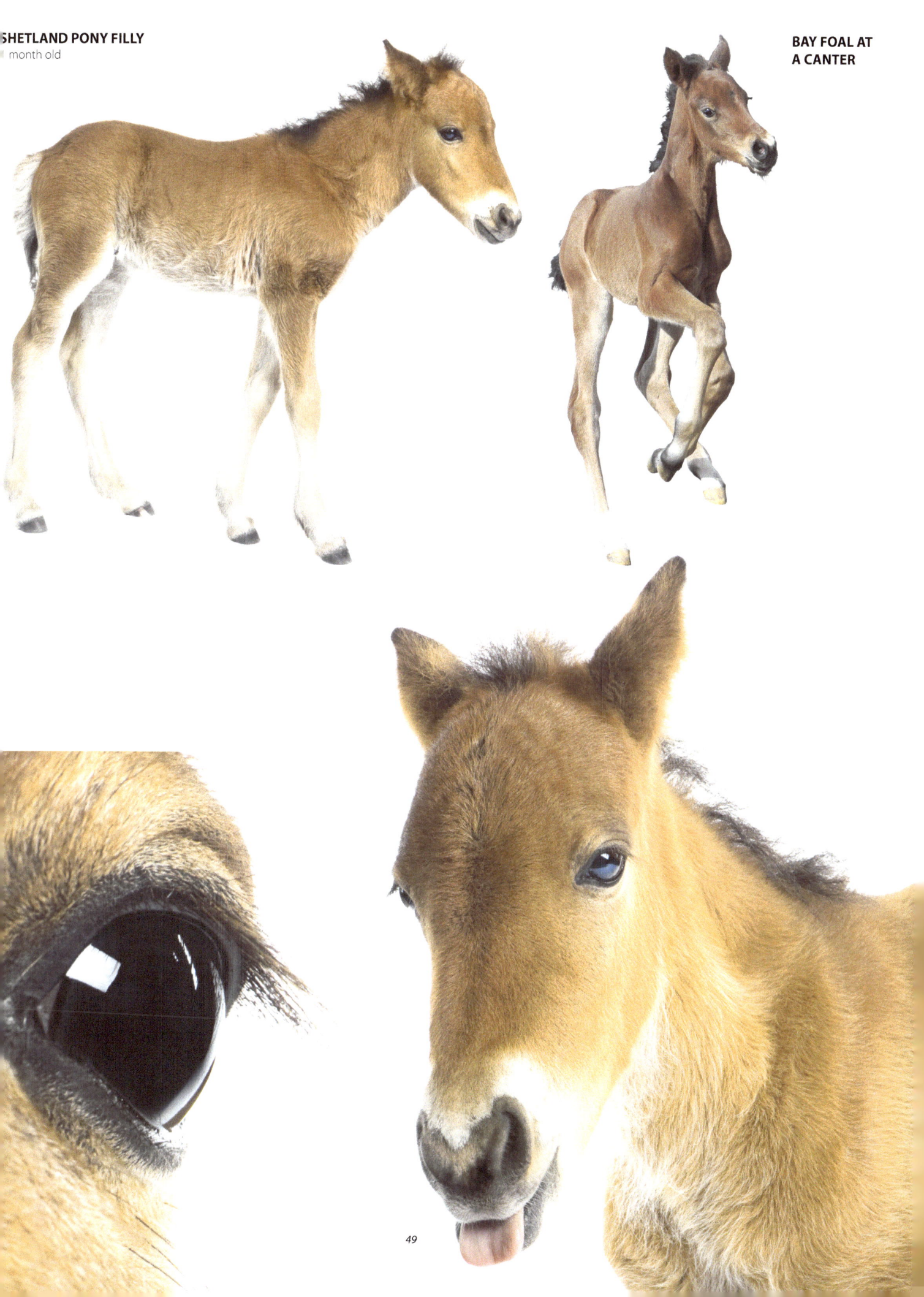

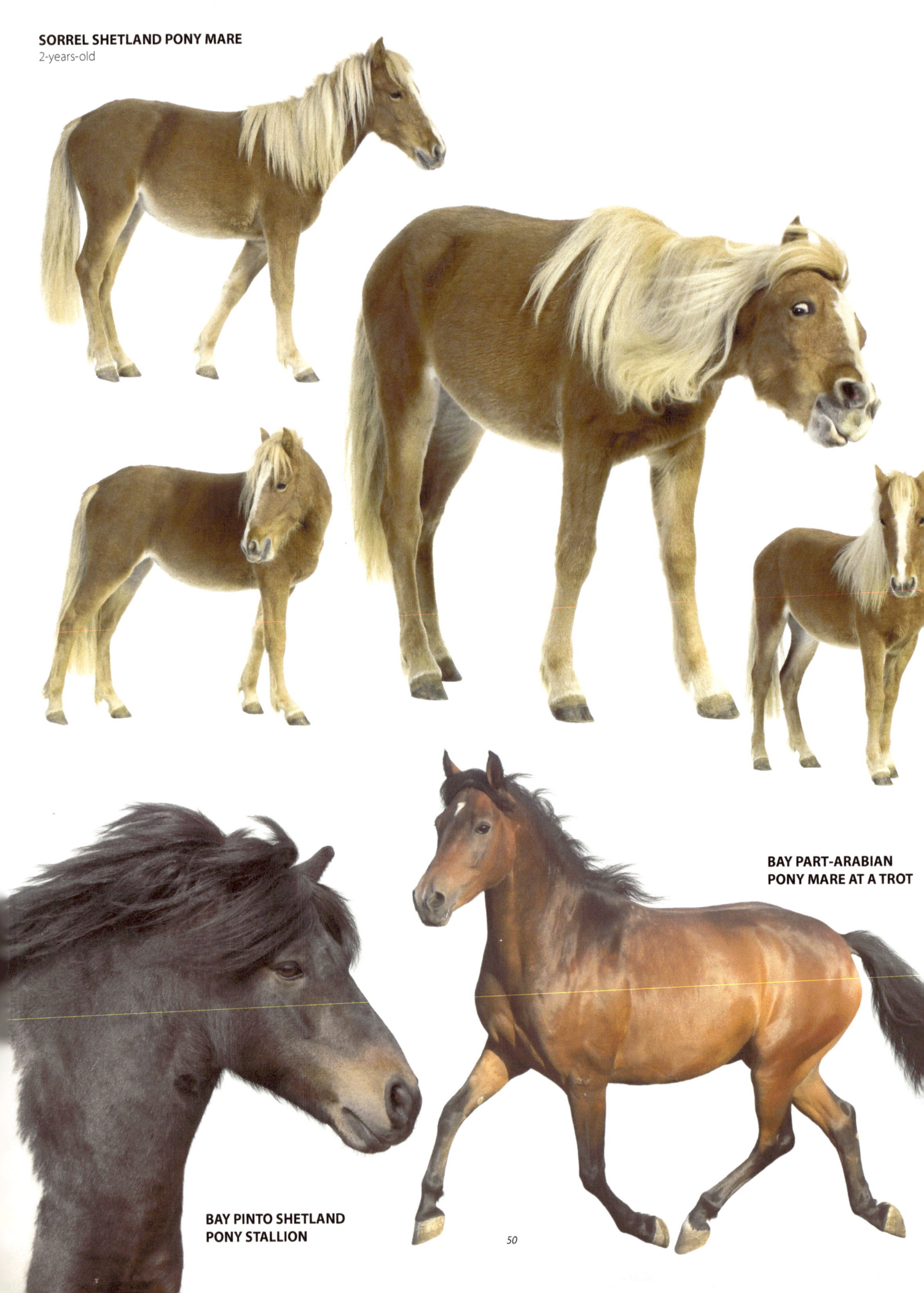

**SORREL SHETLAND PONY MARE**
2-years-old

**BAY PART-ARABIAN
PONY MARE AT A TROT**

**BAY PINTO SHETLAND
PONY STALLION**

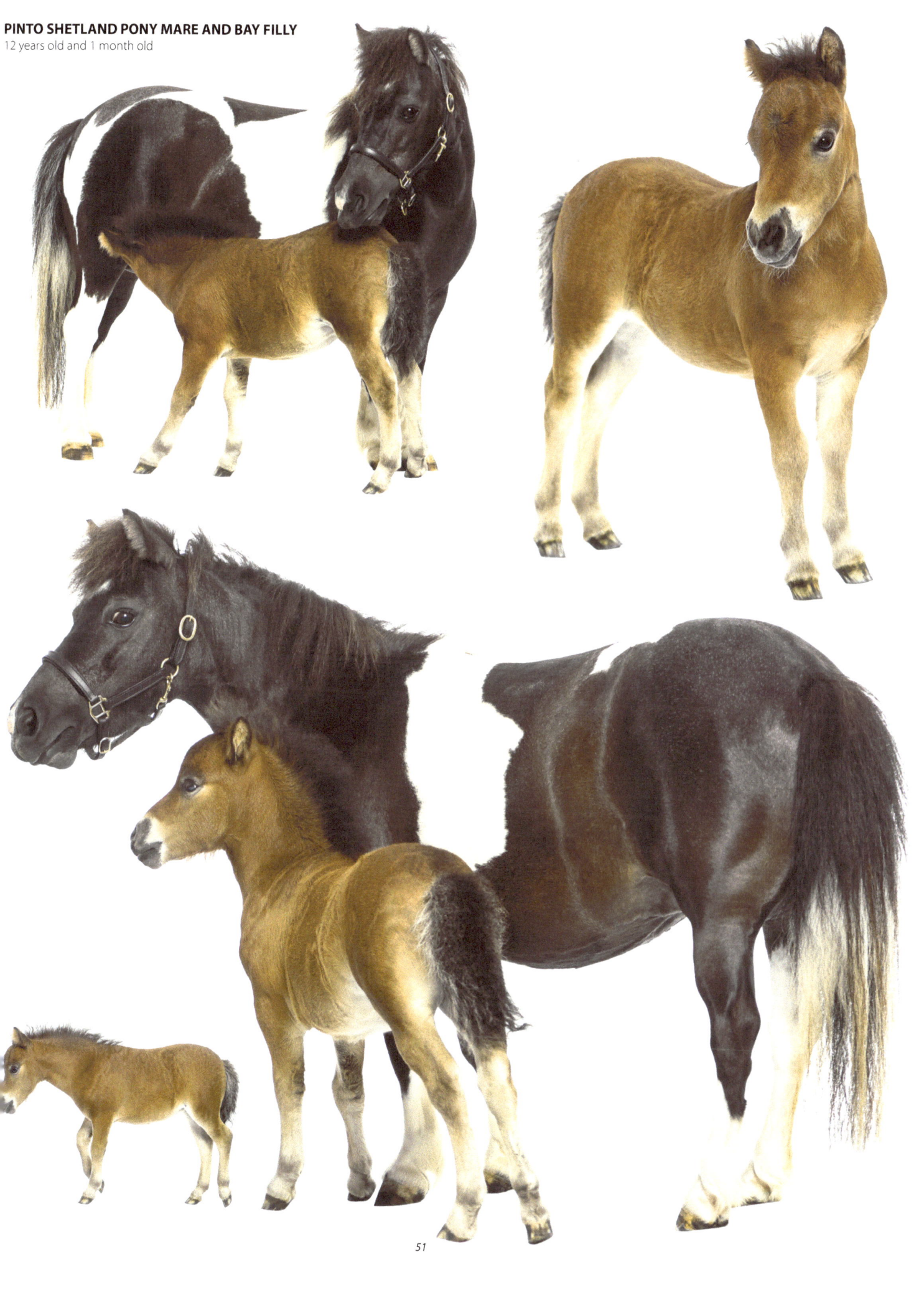

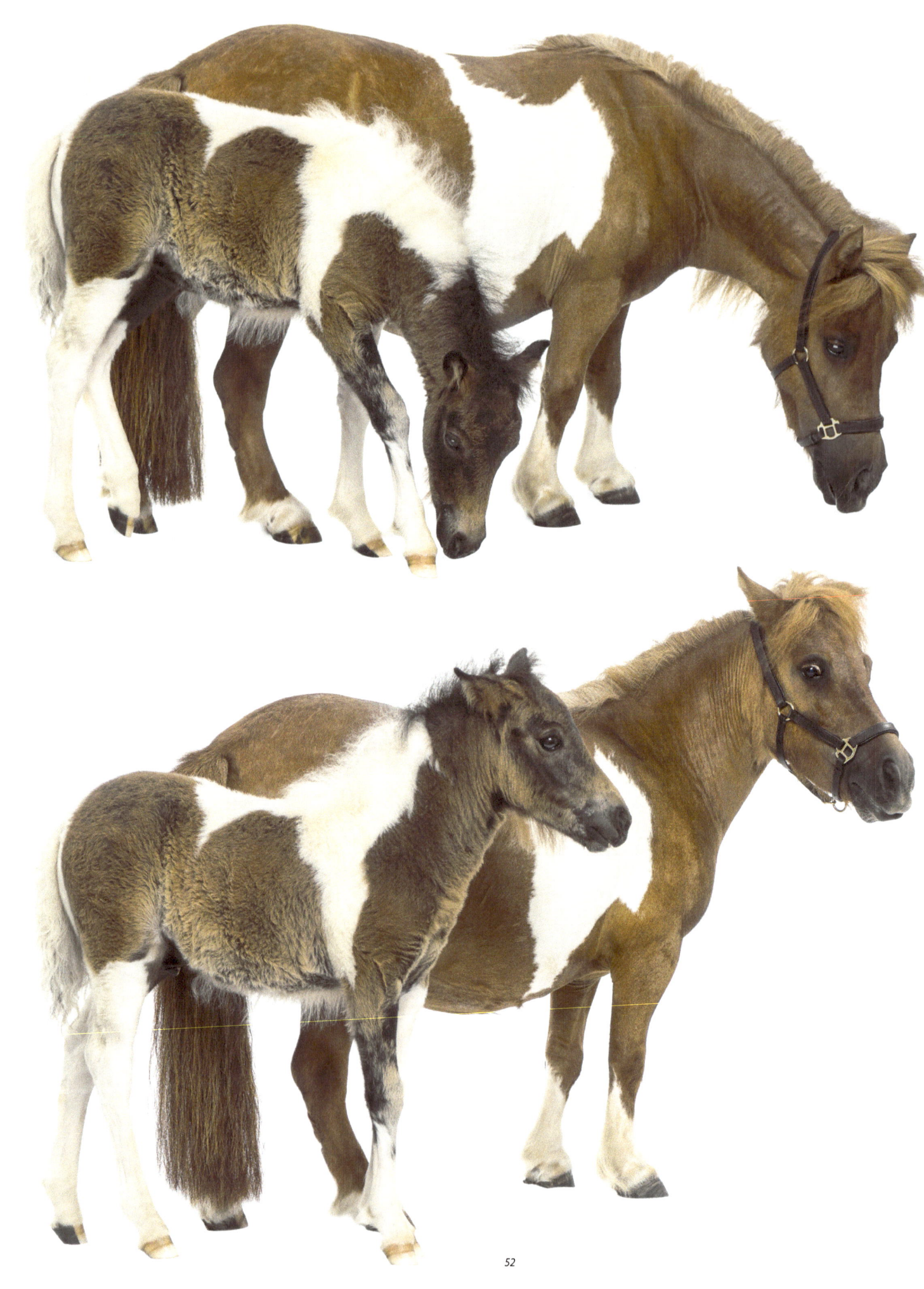

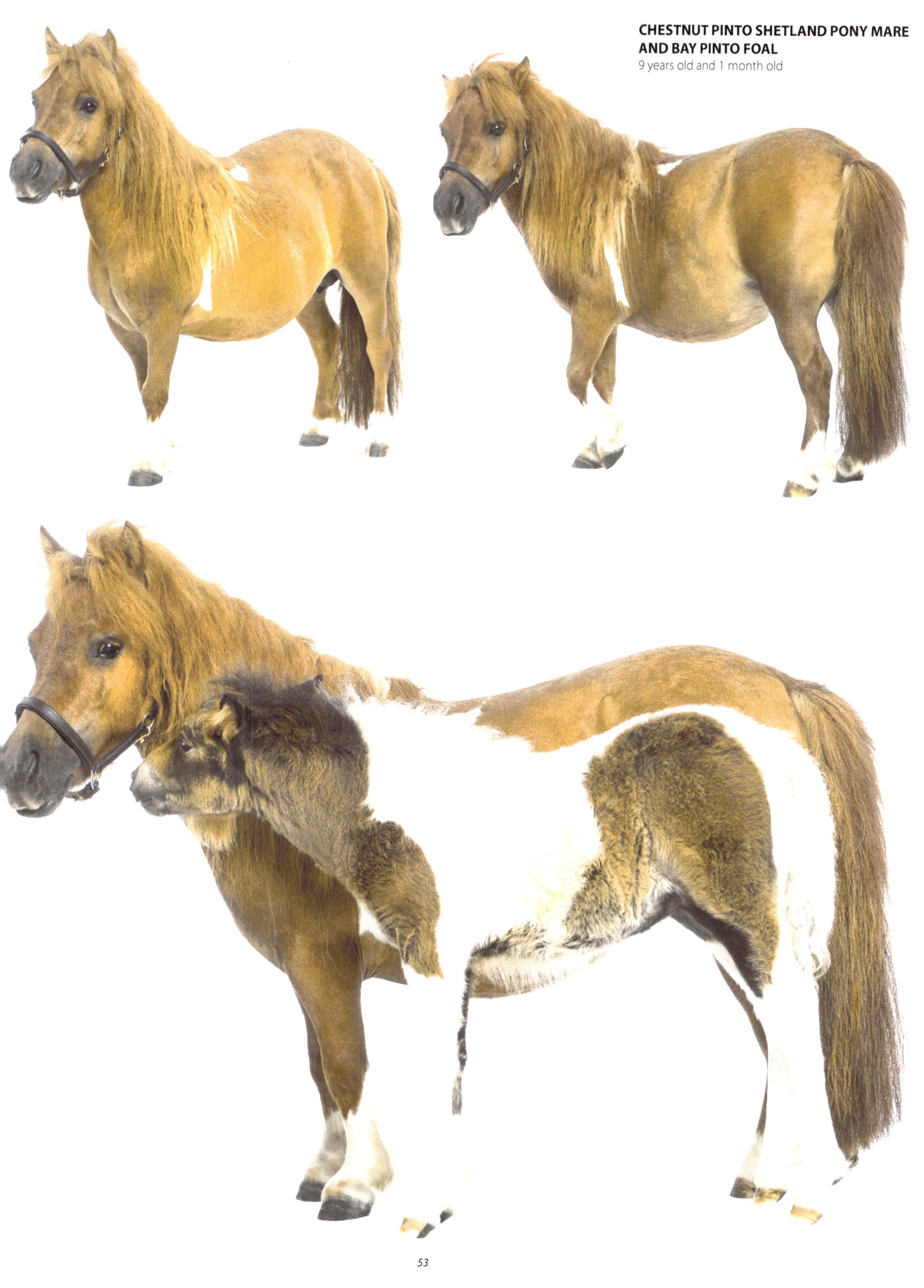

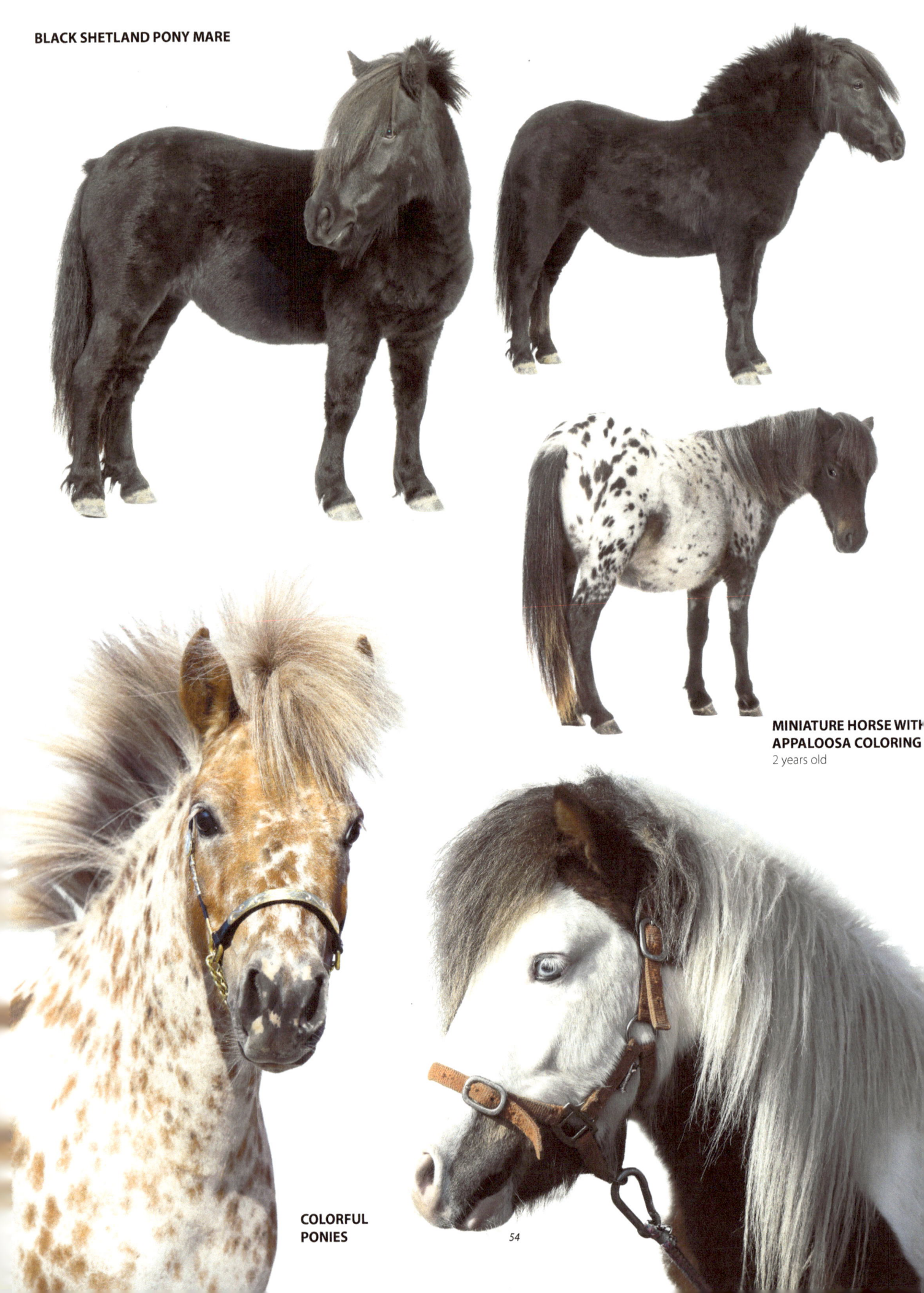

**BLACK SHETLAND PONY MARE**

**MINIATURE HORSE WITH APPALOOSA COLORING**
2 years old

**COLORFUL PONIES**

54

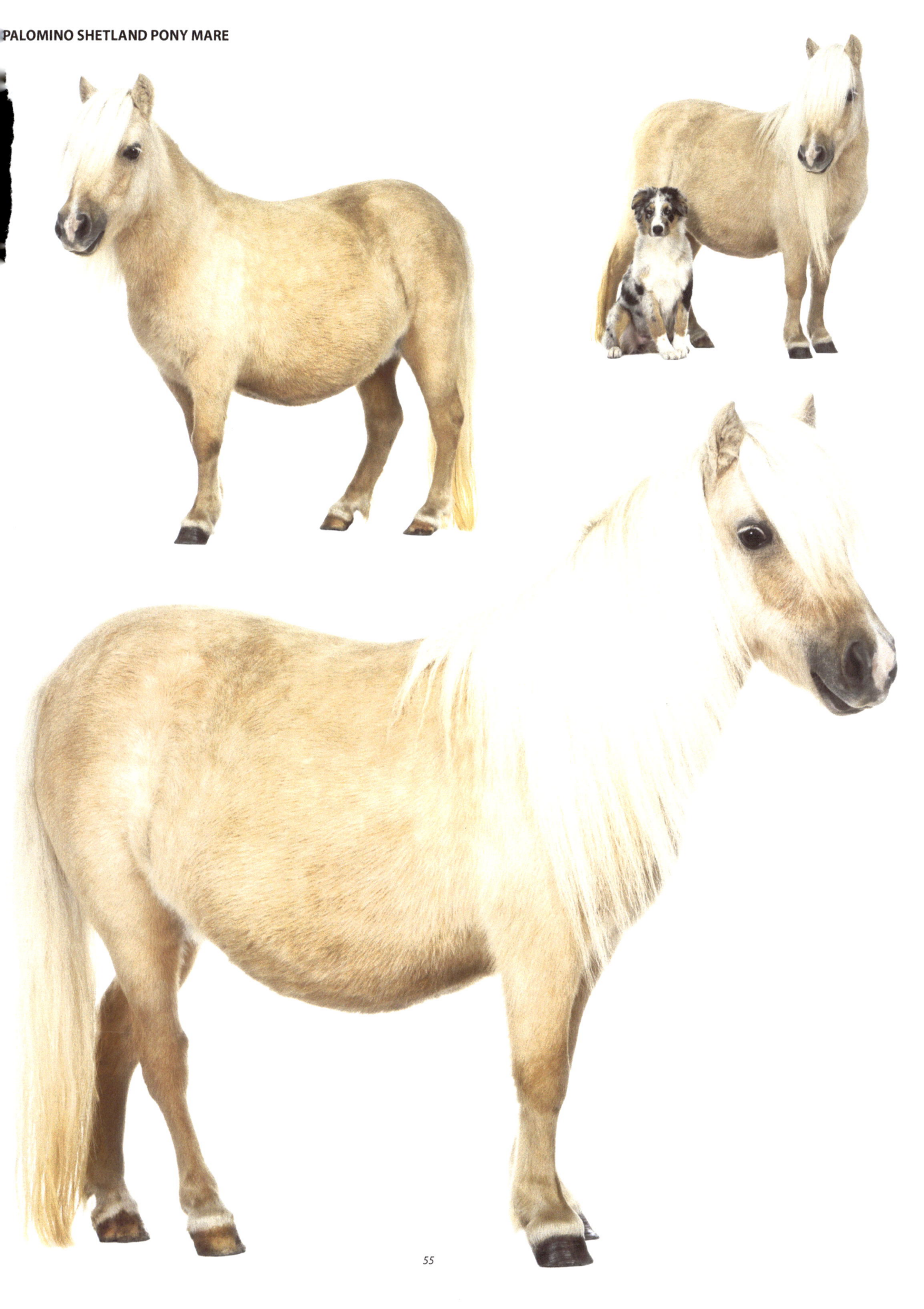

# INDEX

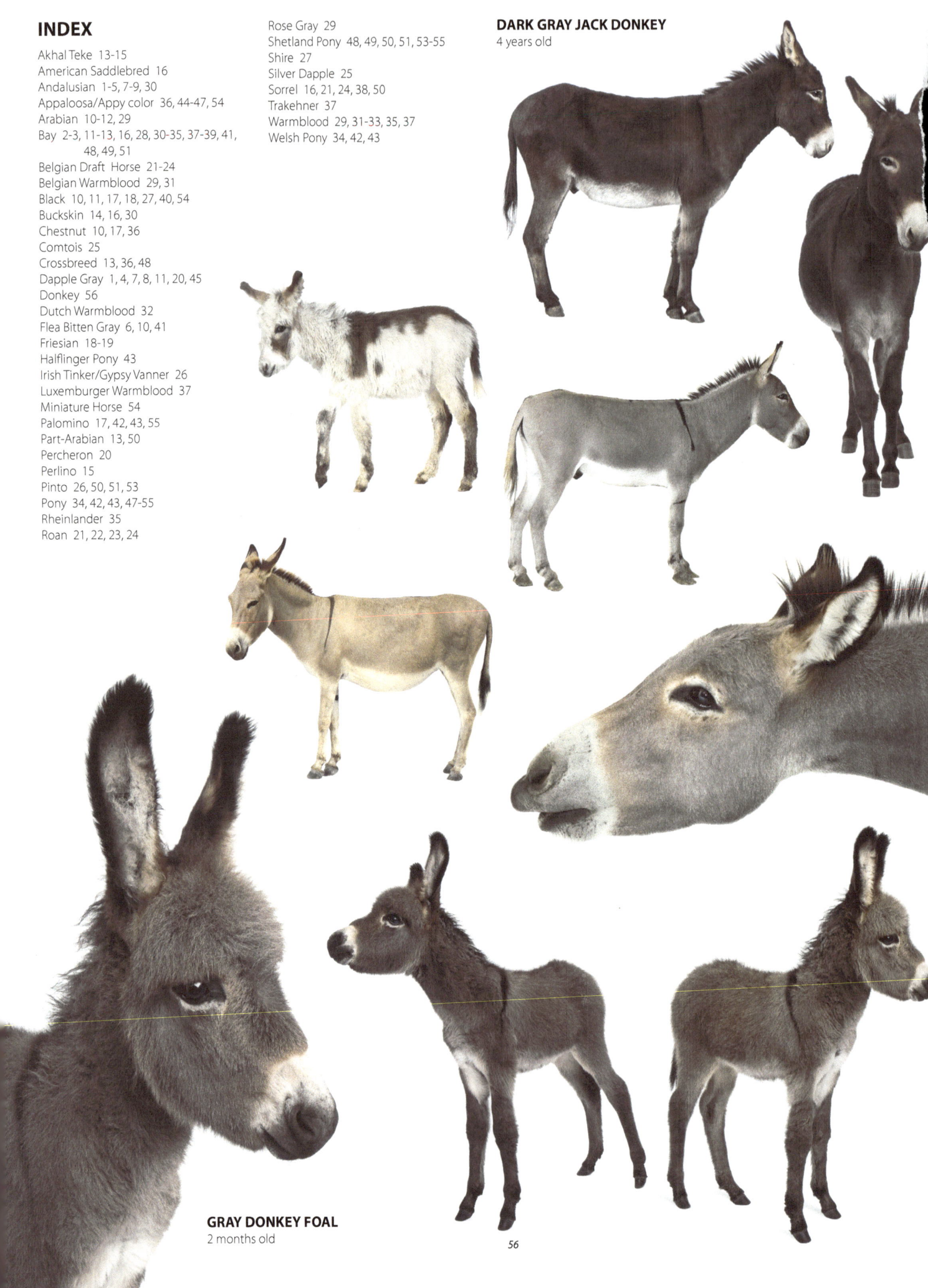

**DARK GRAY JACK DONKEY**
4 years old

**GRAY DONKEY FOAL**
2 months old